ALCOHOL USE AND MISUSE BY YOUNG ADULTS

ALCOHOL USE AND MISUSE BY YOUNG ADULTS

George S. Howard and
Peter E. Nathan, editors

UNIVERSITY OF NOTRE DAME PRESS
NOTRE DAME, INDIANA

Library of Congress Cataloging-in-Publication Data

Alcohol use and misuse by young adults / edited by George S. Howard
and Peter E. Nathan.
        p.   cm.
Includes bibliographical references.
ISBN 0–268–00641–5 (alk. paper)
1. College students—United States—Alcohol use. 2. Young adults—
United States—Alcohol use. 3. Alcoholism—United States—
Prevention. I. Howard, George S. II. Nathan, Peter E.
[DNLM: 1. Alcohol Drinking—epidemiology. 2. Alcohol Drinking—
adverse effects. 3. Alcohol Intoxication—prevention & control.
4. Alcoholism—epidemiology. 5. Students. 6. Student Health
Services—United States. WM 274 A35285 1944]
HV5128.U5A43 1994
362.29'22'0835—dc20
DNLM/DLC
for Library of Congress   93–43478
                                                                      CIP

The paper used in this publication meets the minimum requirements of the
American National Standard for Information Sciences—Permanence of Paper
for Printed Library Materials ANSI Z39.48–1984.

The editors wish to thank the Department of Psychology of the University of Notre Dame and the JM Foundation for supporting the conference that stimulated this book

CONTENTS

EXAMPLES OF EFFECTIVE COLLEGE PROGRAMS

Introduction

George S. Howard and Peter E. Nathan

The typical undergraduate is at a precarious point in his or her development. Having gained most of the physical attributes, intellectual powers, and the social and political rights and responsibilities of adulthood, much is possible and a good deal is expected of these young adults. However, most college students find themselves in an environment where their actions and values are more dominated by their peers than has ever before been the case. If their precollege experiences could be described as being dominated by their families (pre-teen years) and influenced by both family and peers (early teen years), the early adult years spent as college students is likely to be a transition period to independent adulthood. Since this critical stage of development is so influenced by peers, it often appears as a case of the blind muddling along with the blind. But most young adults do manage to muddle through quite nicely. Every year colleges and universities graduate hundreds of thousands of well-educated, responsible, young adults.

While the undergraduate experience is generally a successful developmental experience, for some graduating represents something of a Pyrrhic victory. This is because the manner in which these students dealt with developmental challenges was problematic, and these experiences have left them ill-prepared to deal successfully with future challenges. Inevitably, another substantial portion of each freshmen class fails to graduate. In many such instances, this unhappy outcome becomes an important transition point in what later becomes an unfortunate life story.

While higher education cannot be held responsible for all of the failures of its clientele, it would be irresponsible of educators if they refused to review their failures (and their marginal successes) in an effort to identify common elements

1

that might be related to developmental delays and defeats that take place during the undergraduate years. Virtually every such retrospective analysis by educators finds alcohol misuse an important element in many of these failures.

Alcohol misuse is probably responsible for more academic failure than any other single cause. The eighteen-year-old who has always before had, literally or figuratively, a loving parent looking over his or her shoulder, warning against the evils of alcohol, is especially vulnerable to the peer pressure to drink—and to drink heavily—once he or she has begun attending college away from home. Peer pressure to drink abusively is especially intense when the social life of the undergraduate, as it too often does, revolves around alcohol-energized social events on or off campus.

Beyond the consequences of hangover "the day after," which all too often interferes with class attendance and class performance, heavy drinking frequently prevents students from doing the studying they must do after class if they are to pass their courses. When the choice is between a social event involving alcohol and an evening of studying, it is usually the studying, not the drinking, that is foregone.

Heavy drinkers—often members of fraternities, which exert especially intense pressures on initiates to become "one of the boys" by drinking heavily—risk more than academic failure. Drinking in college is often associated with driving, the combination of which leads both to arrests for drunken driving and, much more serious, injury and death in alcohol-related automobile accidents. Physical violence, by and toward fellow college students, which includes date and acquaintance rape, is also a byproduct of maladaptive drinking by students.

Is it any wonder that collegiate administrators take alcohol consumption by their students as seriously as they do? Few behaviors on campus have alcohol's potential to diminish—or destroy—a college career.

Alcohol use and misuse are complex and multifaceted phenomena. The problems involving alcohol cannot be understood from a single intellectual perspective. Unless one becomes aware of the numerous biological, psychological, and social factors in alcohol use (as well as their complex interactions with one another), one will have an overly simplistic grasp of the tremendous developmental challenges involved in successfully achieving the responsible use of alcohol. The first section of this book reminds the reader of some of the psychological, biological, and social factors that must be considered before one can evaluate programs that might reduce the incidence of failures in higher education attributable in part to alcohol.

The first chapter—Why Won't They Let Us Help Them?—is by Peter E. Nathan. Professor Nathan was the Director of the Center of Alcohol Studies at Rutgers University before he assumed his current post as Provost at the University of Iowa. Nathan's paper helps us appreciate the scope of the problem that alcohol represents for college students, faculty, and administrators and dramatically demonstrates that alcohol can impact young adults in ways that make failing out of school benign by comparison. By uncovering many of the developmental, psychological, social, institutional, legal, and moral issues that attend any institutional stance or program to alter drinking behavior on campus, Nathan sets the stage for many of the issues wrestled with in subsequent chapters.

Next, James W. Smith, the Chief Medical Officer at Schick Shadel Hospital in Seattle, Washington, carefully reviews the medical research related to the biological bases of alcohol misuse. There is great controversy in the field as to whether alcohol misuse and abuse are best understood as biologically based disease processes or as socially learned maladaptive habits. Some "either-or" arguments—such as the disease or habit controversy—have proven to be fruitful, intellectual exchanges. But the polarization such discussions typically produce has generally proven detrimental to the substance abuse field, just as similar, simplistic "either-or" dichotomies have crippled scholarly discourse in other domains (e.g., masculinity or femininity [Constantinople, 1973]; nature versus nurture [Plomin, 1990]; free will or determinism [May, 1981]; innocent versus guilty [Howard, 1992a]). Smith sidesteps these contentious

debates in the alcohol studies field, and instead carefully reviews the scientific literature that suggests biological bases for
human reactions to ethyl alcohol as well as the phenomenon of
addiction. As the history of earlier "either-or" dichotomies has
shown, the truth about alcohol misuse is best understood as a
set of complex interdependencies among biological realities
and learned behavior patterns, rather than as mutually exclusive combatants set against one another in stark dualities.

The final chapter of the first section situates the place of
alcohol in the context of the university's role in the broadly
construed, moral education of young adults. Kevin McDonnell
is professor of philosophy at Saint Mary's College, Notre Dame,
Indiana. Stressing that the moral and educational imperatives
of colleges and universities extend far beyond their legal
obligations to their students, this chapter challenges us to
consider alcohol use and misuse from a moral and broadly
developmental perspective. Professor McDonnell believes it is
insufficient for educators and administrators to adopt policies
and implement programs that merely see to it that laws of the
state and country are not violated. Grounding his arguments in
the tradition of virtue ethics, he challenges us to honor our
commitment to educate the whole person in the stance we take
toward the role of alcohol.

Alcohol misuse represents a serious problem on most
college campuses, but progress has been made toward the
development of more responsible drinking patterns (whether
through moderate drinking or abstinence) by college students.
Much can be learned about what perspectives and practices help
young adults deal more effectively with alcohol consumption
by studying examples of successful helping programs. The second
section—Characteristics of Effective Helping Programs—seeks to
glean wisdom from three rather different programs of research
and treatment of alcohol use and misuse.

William R. Miller is professor of psychology and Director,
Research Division, Center on Alcoholism, Substance Abuse,
and Addictions at the University of New Mexico, Albuquerque,

New Mexico. Miller and Sanchez consider motivating young adults for treatment and lifestyle change to be a task of paramount importance for successful programs. Effectively enhancing motivation is best accomplished when one attends to (and maximizes) six critical elements that influence a young adult's motivation to change. This chapter lays out a comprehensive program to increase students' awareness of the risks inherent in hazardous drinking and drug use practices and to provide a variety of response alternatives through which change might be pursued. This direct translation of psychological theory into a promising, comprehensive alcohol education and treatment program reminds one of Gordon Allport's famous observation that there is nothing so practical as a good theory.

G. Alan Marlatt, professor of psychology and Director of the Addictive Behaviors Research Center, University of Washington, wrote the second chapter in this section with three of his students. These four authors begin by observing that college students in our society will drink—but that drinking can be done either safely or in an unsafe manner. This University of Washington team then proceeds to probe the efficacy of training students in skills-based approaches to avoid the more dangerous aspects of alcohol consumption. This chapter reminds one of Professor McDonnell's point that higher education ought to be education for the challenges to be faced in life. Since drinking is a part of the life of many Americans, part of the responsibility of higher education might be conceived as showing students how to make responsible drinking a component of a virtuous life. This chapter carefully lays out and reviews programs of research that demonstrate that responsible drinking skills can be taught, are cost-effective, and represent effective forms of secondary prevention of alcohol misuse.

Alcoholics Anonymous (A.A.) has undoubtedly become the most widely used program to remediate of alcoholism. For this reason, much can be learned about recovery from alcohol misuse by examining the A.A. experience. John E. Keller, now actively retired at the Zion Lutheran Church in Johnson, Nebraska, was for many years the President and Chief Clinical Officer of Parkside Lutheran Hospital. Keller offers an unusual view of the founding and history of the A.A. movement. He highlights the role that spirituality has always played in A.A. programs of recovery, and how the regnant medical and psychological communities have found the spiritual aspect of A.A.'s program (coupled with its undeniable success in promoting recovery of alcoholics) difficult to accept. What might be sensed as a vague tension in the previous chapters becomes a palpable force in Keller's chapter. One's understanding of alcohol misuse, prevention, and treatment programs is molded by one's vision of the nature of human beings—and of the nature of science.

The discussion of alcohol use and misuse to this point in the book has been largely grounded in Enlightenment views of human nature and science. Enlightenment (also called Modernist) thought springs from the seventeenth-century Baconian revolution in science. It is committed to a form of rationality that seeks to combine sensory experience with mathematical reasoning in seeking knowledge. Enlightenment thinking holds a deep suspicion of nonscientific traditions (especially religions) and ways of knowing that it brands as superstitions. The book's chapters to this point square well with Enlightenment assumptions about human nature and the scientific study of alcohol. However, since our notion, "the scientific," is partially defined in contradistinction to "the religious," Keller's thoughts on the role of spirituality in treatment might strike some readers as out of place in this volume. The Romanticist tradition of the sixteenth century has always served as a counterpoint to Enlightenment strains in our intellectual traditions. Unlike Enlightenment thought, Romanticist thought prizes the complexity and diversity of human life for its own sake—not as something to be transcended or explained away by theoretical or scientific thought. Romanticists emphasize the virtue of empathic understanding of the person and revel in the individual's uniqueness and idiosyncrasies. Some (e.g., Howard,

1992b, Toulmin, 1990) blame the current postmodern crisis of confidence in society on our inability to successfully integrate Enlightenment and Romanticist modes of thought into a holistic vision of human nature. That is, the postmodern crisis is *not* upon us because the foundations of Modernism (grounded in Enlightenment thought) have been completely discredited and are in need of replacement by another (as yet unknown) tradition. Rather, the postmodern crisis can be seen as the reassertion of the importance of Romanticist themes, and the need to integrate these insights with Enlightenment perspectives into a holistic intellectual tradition. From this perspective, the postmodern crisis can be seen as the birth pains for an integration of Romanticist and Enlightenment traditions that has been sorely needed, but gone begging, for almost three hundred years.

Keller's paper casts us upon the horns of the postmodern dilemma. Peppered with nonscientific concepts like spirituality, forgiveness, grace, repentance, and the like, one wonders what such an approach can offer our emerging scientific understanding of alcohol misuse and treatment. Although the chapter (and indeed the entire history of A.A.) has a great deal to offer to a holistic scientific understanding of the human experience with alcohol, the experience (and wisdom) of Romantic humanists will be difficult for scientists to assimilate because the insights result from language systems and traditions that are so different from their own. With the perspective furnished by Keller's chapter, the reader can now sense the outlines of a broader, holistic understanding of the problem of alcohol consumption in earlier chapters (by, for example, Nathan and McDonnell) as warnings to the alcohol studies field not to have its understanding of human nature and the phenomenon of alcohol misuse circumscribed by (and held hostage to) our Enlightenment assumptions. Like all of post-modern society, the alcohol studies field is struggling to integrate insights that have been garnered from disparate (often antagonistic) intellectual perspectives. Many of the current controversies among addictionologists were not created *de novo* by the field. Rather, the controversies were inherited from long-standing antimonies in our broader intellectual traditions. Essays such as Keller's offer opportunities for those of us who are steeped in Modernist perspectives to broaden our vision of human nature. That is, we might use this occasion as an opportunity to come to know ourselves as human beings even more fully.

Any treatment of alcohol use and misuse can be situated along many dimensions simultaneously. If one were to think of this book with respect to the generality versus specificity of the treatment of issues and suggestions, the first section would be seen as more general than the second section, where analyses and recommendations become ever more specific and concrete. The third section of the present book pushes this trend even further. The section entitled Examples of Effective College Programs deals with programs currently in place at Dartmouth University, Brown University, and Rutgers University. Where the first two sections dealt with global issues of alcohol use and misuse as well as the molar characteristics of effective educational and treatment programs, the level of discourse precluded dealing with the specifics of establishing and fine-tuning such programs. By contrast, this third section deals with a range of pragmatic considerations of three multifaceted, comprehensive programs. Many parts of these programs might benefit institutions in higher education and their clientele.

Jean W. Kinney's field of specialization is social work, and she serves as Director of the Project Cork Institute at the Dartmouth Medical School, Hanover, New Hampshire. Kinney champions a primary prevention vision designed to deal with a problem *before* it occurs. In the words we've all memorized, but typically fail to heed, "An ounce of prevention is worth a pound of cure." Picking up on themes traced earlier by Miller, Marlatt and their co-authors, Kinney first answers the typical objections to campus programs designed to prevent alcohol misuse. Next, the chapter traces the specific features possessed by successful, comprehensive programs of alcohol education. Finally, the author identifies process considerations as the elements that are typically neglected and therefore responsible for the failure (or only limited success) of some programs that seek to aid students in becoming less susceptible to problems of alcohol misuse. Kinney provides helpful detail on the roles that various groups (faculty, administration, alumni, the personnel department, the athletic department, campus police, etc.) might play to engineer a milieu in which students might develop effective personal styles to help them navigate the dangerous shoals of alcohol use.

The experience at Brown University is explicated for us by Bruce E. Donovan, a Professor of Classics, who specializes in issues of chemical dependency in his work as Associate Dean of the College. Donovan's chapter is unique in that it traces a comprehensive alcohol education and treatment program completely integrated into all the normal offices and programs of the university. Brown's approach is *not* to establish a completely new office on campus for campus alcohol problems. Donovan describes a strategy by which a regular faculty member is charged with coordinating the efforts of the entire university community so that each of the relevant parts of the community does its part in solving the university's challenge of proper alcohol education and treatment. Continuing several discussions initiated in the previous chapter, Donovan grapples with real issues that motivate and impede change on college campuses. He wrestles with the real, idiosyncratic values and ambitions that determine the success and failure of any program on campus. More than other chapters, Kinney and Donovan offer concrete advice on how to manage alcohol prevention and treatment programs in order to afford these efforts the best possible chance of success in their institutional milieus.

The final chapter of this section is by Barbara S. McCrady, Professor of Psychology and Clinical Director of the Center of Alcohol Studies, Rutgers University in Piscataway, New Jersey. Because students are likely to be farther away from their homes and families than ever before in their lives, university agencies can tend to underestimate the importance of families in both the genesis and remediation of problems of alcohol misuse. In emphasizing the importance of social networks (e.g., the family, dormitory mates, special interest groups such as theater, athletics, etc.) in alcohol use, misuse, and treatment, McCrady reminds us that students do not live in social vacuums. Further, in reviewing the research literature on the relative efficacy of various treatment approaches (e.g., behavioral, disease model, family systems, psychopharmacological), she makes the important point that effectively changing humans' actions in one domain often involves making alterations in several areas of their lives to maximize the chances that enduring habits will change (see Lazarus' 1981, 1985 multimodal therapy) and to reduce the chances that backsliding into old habits will occur (see Marlatt & Gordon's 1985 work on relapse prevention).

In looking at two different comprehensive education and treatment programs in detail (Dartmouth University and Brown University) and considering four others more sketchily (Rutgers University, University of New Mexico, University of Washington, and Alcoholics Anonymous), we gain a sense of the tremendous diversity among programs in the alcohol area. Every program ought to be tailored to the unique needs, strengths, and mission of its institution. Few programs remain unchanged over time. Development in programs in response to their experiences within changing institutions, within our ever-changing society, is inevitable and highly desirable. Providing a panoply of program options in this volume should stimulate experimentation with programs to meet currently underserved institutional needs, and recognition of directions in which current programs might choose to evolve in order to better serve our student, faculty, administration, alumni, and other clienteles.

These chapters reveal the extent and complexity of what we now know about alcohol misuse's causes and treatments, as well as about efforts to prevent it in young adults of college age. We know a great deal more about each of these topics now than we did as recently as a decade ago, so rapid and intense has been the quest to acquire and apply this knowledge. Yet, for all that we know, there is much that remains beyond our understanding at present. As a consequence, this book is as revealing in many ways for what it discloses about what we have still to learn about destructive drinking by young adults as it is for what it shows we now understand.

We know a great deal more about biologically and genetically based etiologic factors and much more about the role of learning in alcohol use and abuse than we did ten or twenty years ago. Nonetheless, we do not yet know how biology and genetics are *mediated* in the expression of misuse: Are craving, the need to self-medicate, ultra-rapid tolerance or some other behavior the means by which biological and genetic factors influence alcohol misuse? In like fashion, as we review the plethora of studies on learning's impact on misuse, we must admit that we still do not know whether abusive drinking is most often directly modeled, whether what is learned of greatest relevance to misuse is the set of attitudes or expectancies about alcohol's impact that is characteristic of the abuser, or whether other modes of learning are involved singly or in combination.

Similarly, although we now know that motivational factors, interpersonal influence, and the degree of match between patient and treatment milieu are all important factors in successful treatment, designing the most effective treatment for the single abusing individual is still beyond our grasp.

Finally, although we know that prevention is far more cost-effective than treatment, even when it is begun a decade or more before the individual is at greatest risk to develop abusive drinking practices, and although we know how to increase an individual's alcohol-related information and attitudes, the impact of prevention programs on actual rates of alcoholism remains surprisingly modest.

As you read the chapters that follow, then, we encourage you to pay close attention to what their authors say has been achieved—as well as what remains to be achieved. Doing so will give you a sense for the great excitement and turmoil in a field which has come far in a short time, but which nonetheless has more distance to cover before it has the crucial answers it seeks.

References

Constantinople, A. P. (1973). Masculinity-femininity: An exception to a famous dictum? *Psychological Bulletin, 80,* 389–407.

Howard, G. S. (1992a). No middle voice. *Theoretical and Philosophical Psychology, 12,* 12–26.

Howard, G. S. (1992b). Behold our creation! What counseling psychology has become, and might yet become. *Journal of Counseling Psychology, 39,* 406–434.

Lazarus, A. A. (1981). *The practice of multimodal therapy.* New York: McGraw-Hill.

Lazarus, A. A. (1985). *Casebook of multimodal therapy.* New York: Guilford Press.

Marlatt, G. A., & Gordon, J. R. (Eds.) (1985). *Relapse prevention: Maintenance strategies in the treatment of addictive behaviors.* New York: Guilford Press.

May, R. (1981). *Freedom and destiny.* New York: Norton.

Plomin, R. (1990). *Nature and nurture: An introduction to human behavioral genetics.* Pacific Grove, Calif.: Brooks/Cole.

Toulmin, S. (1990). *Cosmopolis: The hidden agenda of modernity.* New York: The Free Press.

PART I

WHY WON'T THEY LET US HELP THEM ?

Unanswered Questions about Distressed Faculty, Staff and Students: Why Won't They Let Us Help Them ?

Peter E. Nathan

A short time ago, Rutgers University suffered a grievous loss. It was caused by alcohol, it was unnecessary, and it has led Rutgers students, faculty, and administrators to begin an intensive period of self-examination. It is possible that something good may come of this tragedy.

An eighteen-year-old fraternity pledge died from acute alcohol intoxication on the night he was to be initiated into the fraternity. Forced to consume more than twenty "Kamikazees" in less than an hour (a Kamikazee is a potent mixture of vodka and the liqueur Triple Sec), the young man died a few hours later with a blood alcohol concentration substantially in excess of 0.45 mg/dl. (This lethal blood alcohol concentration amounts to more than four times the legal limit of intoxication for drinking drivers, which is 0.10 mg/dl!) A fellow pledge would also have died with about the same blood alcohol concentration had not friends taken him to the hospital somewhat earlier.

Rutgers has closed down the young victim's fraternity, at least for the time being, banned campus-wide all fraternity social functions involving alcohol, and launched an intensive investigation of the role of fraternities and sororities in the life of Rutgers undergraduates. The county prosecutor, following a thorough investigation of the incident, will determine whether and whom to indict.

Why didn't the officers of the fraternity obey carefully wrought university regulations surrounding the serving of

15

alcohol? Why did they serve alcohol to underage members, including the entire group of pledges? Why did they force their pledges to drink amounts of alcohol that placed them at great risk? For that matter, why did Rutgers University suffer this trauma? Rutgers is acknowledged (by many in a position to know) to have developed one of the nation's first, strongest, and most effective alcohol programs.

Why won't they let us help them?

Originally, this chapter was to be informed by three data sources: first, by my years of experience in treating men and women impaired by alcohol and drugs, second, by my more recent involvement in efforts to develop treatment programs for distressed professionals, and third, by my immersion in the extensive empirical and clinical literature on this subject (e.g., Nathan, 1983, 1984b, 1985). My presentation was to have addressed the question, "Why won't distressed faculty and staff let us help them?"

But the recent unhappy events at Rutgers and my subsequent appointment to a university-wide committee of faculty, students, and administrators charged with looking into reasons for what now seems clearly widespread alcohol misuse by students in New Brunswick, especially by members of Rutgers fraternities, leads me to broaden the scope of this chapter. Accordingly, I will ask—and then try to answer—the following question: Why do faculty, staff, and students, individually and collectively, so regularly and so effectively resist our efforts to help them avoid alcohol misuse?

This expanded scope makes sense for another reason. It enables consideration of the striking, extremely instructive commonalities among faculty, staff, and students in their responses both to their own alcohol use and misuse and to that of others. These commonalities, which are rarely acknowledged, deserve discussion because they almost certainly contribute to the problem.

I will refer frequently to Rutgers faculty, staff, and students because I know them best and because the recent events at

Rutgers have brought this issue to sharp focus. I do not refer to them because they are more likely than faculty, staff, and students in other universities to misuse alcohol or resist efforts at treatment or prevention. There is no reason to believe that Rutgers is much different from other public universities of its size in the nature and extent of the alcohol and drug problems. There is every reason to believe, however, that a careful examination of the manner in which Rutgers faculty, staff, and students have dealt with these problems may be instructive for faculty, staff, and students at a wide variety of other universities.

Many of those who have worked most closely with alcohol abusers have noted the tendency on the part of many, including those most sorely afflicted, to minimize or deny the nature and extent of their problems with alcohol (Blume, 1980; Pattison, 1985). This feature of alcoholic behavior is seen as both antecedent to and consequent of the disorder by many members of Alcoholics Anonymous, whose *Twelve Steps* prescribe successful confrontation with denial as a precursor to recovery from alcoholism. While the tendency to deny serious illness is not restricted to the alcoholic, the effort to minimize alcohol problems appears to represent an especially serious impediment to the successful treatment of chronic alcoholics, the persons who most often come to the attention of self-help groups like A.A.

Of more relevance to the issues at hand, denial also plays a central role in the difficulties we experience in trying to convince persons in the university community who have just gotten into trouble with alcohol—or are at heightened risk to do so—to let us help them. Let me illustrate.

Despite intensive efforts for several years to alert them to the perils of alcohol misuse, officers and members of Rutgers fraternities have persisted in condoning, in many instances encouraging, heavy drinking during pledging and at social functions. This behavior has been maintained in the face of clear legal sanctions against underage drinking and the obvious risks that drinking of this magnitude involves. It also persists in the face of the university's strong and persistent efforts to educate students about the problems of alcohol misuse. It seems clear that denial and minimization play important roles in the students' cavalier attitude toward alcohol.

But it wasn't just the students who deluded themselves about alcohol at Rutgers. Faculty and staff responsible for working with students knew how frequently fraternities at Rutgers center their social activities around substantial alcohol use—but did not act on this knowledge. Why did they fail to prevent the recent alcohol-related death, given this awareness? In part, because the widespread misuse of alcohol by students at universities is typically viewed as inevitable, "because that's the way it's always been," especially among fraternity members, for whom alcohol has always represented a special test of manhood and a specific confirmation of fraternity.

Some administrators at Rutgers also denied the ubiquity of alcohol misuse on campus by blaming the fraternities for all alcohol problems at the university. In viewing the fraternities' focus on drinking as the principal cause of the problem, they could ignore or deny a problem of only slightly lesser magnitude among residents of dormitories.

The existence of a comprehensive alcohol policy at Rutgers convinced still other faculty and administrators that the problem of alcohol misuse had already been dealt with, even while they failed to test out this assumption and continued to reassure themselves that the problem was essentially solved.

Denying, minimizing, and otherwise distorting the difficulty with which alcohol misuse problems are prevented or solved is hardly the exclusive province of Rutgers' faculty, staff, and students. Many others, including many mental health professionals, who presumably should know better, share that unfortunate tendency.

For example, when the members of the governance structure of the American Psychological Association were advised to follow the example of other professions and develop a comprehensive national program for distressed psychologists, a variety of negative reactions were elicited that suggested a surprising lack of accurate information about the problem

(Kilberg, Nathan, & Thoreson, 1986; Nathan, 1982; Thoreson et al., 1983). A common theme expressed by association members most strongly opposed to the program was that psychologists are better able than other professionals either to avoid or to confront successfully the problems of alcohol and drug misuse and that, as a consequence, the program would never be cost effective. This belief was maintained by many in the face of substantial data to the contrary (Nathan, 1986).

Some of the most influential voices in the New Jersey Dental Society, though fortunately not a majority, had come to a similar conclusion by the time that group was asked to sponsor a program to deal with their distressed colleagues in 1984. Happily, that misinformation was successfully disputed by Barbara McCrady, who continues to oversee the program, now a very successful one, on behalf of the Center of Alcohol Studies at Rutgers.

The extent to which corporate managers are able to convince themselves that their employees do not suffer from the consequences of alcohol misuse, despite clear evidence to the contrary, is also instructive and quite surprising (Nathan, 1984a). A meeting with two senior officers of a large bank in Philadelphia, at which the question of the establishment of an employee assistance program was discussed, comes to mind. In justifying his decision not to allocate the resources necessary to establish the EAP, the president of the bank asserted that he knew of no alcohol problems among any employee of the bank. He made this statement even though the recent months had seen three suicides by mid-level managers, at least two of them clearly alcohol-related. This man was not lying; he had simply convinced himself, against the data, that alcohol was not a factor in the unhappy events at the bank and that he ought not consider changing his mind.

Some may take a perverse sort of pleasure in the fact that the tragedy at Rutgers stemmed only in part from student denial of the risks associated with alcohol misuse, denial that differed little from that of older and, presumably, wiser heads in and outside the university. Said another way, late adolescents do not monopolize the ranks of those who think wrong-headedly about alcohol.

Why do so many bankers, dentists, psychologists, university faculty, staff, and students fail to heed warnings about alcohol and drug problems from those in a position to know? Why do they think they know better than the experts do? Why can they so easily convince themselves that the dangers of alcohol are for others, not them? And why do so many of us, not just those who are young or in a special risk category, share these fundamental misunderstandings about this drug?

As documented above, denial and self-interest play central roles in this process. Important, as well, is simple ignorance, leavened by misinformation, about alcohol as a drug. The tragic events at Rutgers came about, in part, because the leadership of the fraternity responsible for organizing the fatal installation celebration simply did not know that the consumption of more than twenty ounces of beverage alcohol in an hour or less would result in excessively high blood alcohol levels, levels that entailed the distinct risk of coma and death. Despite the sophisticated alcohol education program to which all students at Rutgers are exposed, despite the special attention the fraternities receive because their members are considered to be at heightened risk for alcohol misuse, these students did not know or did not appreciate the dangers of alcohol as a drug.

There is no reason to believe that faculty and staff at Rutgers are any better informed about alcohol's effects on behavior and health. In talking to Rutgers colleagues about the recent untoward events, I have been reminded again and again of how little accurate information even distinguished researchers in the biological and social sciences have about alcohol, a drug they view very differently, unfortunately, from such substances as heroin, cocaine, and the barbiturates.

How are we to make sense of what seems to be an all-too-successful effort on the part of faculty, staff, students, business men and women, professionals, and others to diminish the threat posed by alcohol and other drugs? Wishful thinking, denial, ignorance, self-interest, all play important roles in the process. As it has been at Rutgers, so it might well be at many other universities.

Why won't they let us help them?

Many of them won't let us help them because they don't believe us, because they don't trust our motives. Why? Perhaps it is because what we say and what we do are not always in synchrony. We are all familiar with the common portrayal of psychiatrists and psychologists as, if anything, more disturbed and less rational than their patients. The stereotype of the maladjusted mental health professional who cannot practice what he or she preaches ought to serve as an especially helpful object lesson for those who work with college students around alcohol and drug problems and issues.

Were I working with students around issues having to do with alcohol use and misuse, I would ask the following questions of myself: Do I model in my own use of alcohol and in my own attitudes toward alcohol the attitudes and behavior I believe the students I work with ought to adopt? Is my own use of alcohol fully informed? Above all, do I create the credibility and the trust that are essential to the acceptance of my teaching?

I believe that the role of the university in helping prepare young adults for the place of alcohol in their lives is no different from the role of the university in helping prepare young adults for the assumption of any other of their future roles in society. Among the best preparation for these roles, in my judgment, is immersion in a four-year liberal arts curriculum. That curriculum exposes the young adult to the accumulated wisdom, which includes both the triumphs and the tragedies, of those who have gone before. Only by knowing what heights humankind has reached, in the arts, the sciences, and the humanities, as well as the depths we have plumbed, the wars we have fought, the ethical and moral lapses of which we have been capable, can young adults make the reasoned ethical and moral choices we expect from educated persons. In this task, being able to share their reactions to this learning with faculty who model wisdom leavened by humanity is, of course, fully as important as the material itself in the learning process.

Having said this much, I am left to ponder whether there is anything additional that the four-year undergraduate experience has to offer vis-à-vis alcohol and drug use. Viewed from the perspective of the developmental process, I have to confess to a certain skepticism that much more can be done in four years that has not already been done in the eighteen years preceding. To this end, those who have concerned themselves with the etiology of alcoholism would conclude that at least two major factors will not be further impacted by the undergraduate experience. These factors are the person's risk status (that is, whether or not he or she has a family history of alcoholism) and the cultural and other environmental influences on drinking to which he or she has been exposed before the age of eighteen.

Of course, peer group influence, by contrast, almost certainly continues to play an important role in determining drinking patterns during the four years of college, just as it did during earlier adolescence. What is uncertain is the extent to which peer influence in college—for example, the pressure to consume substantial quantities of alcohol during the process of pledging a fraternity—plays a role in the etiology of alcohol problems post-college. Unknown as well is the differential role of early and later peer influence. Does peer pressure during college play a greater or a lesser role in alcoholism etiology than peer pressure at an earlier time? I am not aware of empirical data which addresses these interesting questions.

The universities for which I have the greatest respect are those that take most seriously their responsibility to educate undergraduates in the liberal arts, because it is these four years of humane education which best prepare an educated person. A community of scholars best captures what I have in mind. Together, faculty and students examine our liberal heritage, in the process making their own decisions about what has most relevance for their own lives. This kind of teaching and learning requires a good deal more interaction between faculty and students than most multiversities can manage. This kind of education, I believe, is a goal that most liberal arts institutions have set for the four undergraduate years.

Alcohol education, like liberal education, is integral to these years. Part of it derives from student-student relationships, part from student-faculty relationships. The latter ought to focus on how one is to make wise, ethical, and moral choices. Perhaps we ought not to leave this important responsibility solely to the alcohol educators. Perhaps, instead, we ought to expect it from liberal educators as well, men and women capable of teaching the history of drug and alcohol use in the context of their teaching about the history of other moral choices.

Questions about the role of the university in helping prepare young adults for the place of alcohol in their lives? I have a few to propose and a couple of them are decidedly apocryphal!

(1) Are the university's faculty credible when they teach students about moral choices?

(2) Do the faculty at the university who teach about moral choices also model moral choices, in their attitudes and beliefs as well as in their behavior?

(3) Are faculty at the university provided an opportunity to educate themselves on alcohol use and misuse?

(4) Is an alcohol education program for students in place, required, and important to the university community?

(5) Are trained alcohol and drug counselors available to faculty, staff, and students with alcohol and drug problems?

(6) Finally, does the university's prevailing social climate, even on Saturday afternoons in October, permit young men and women easily to abstain from the use of alcohol?

References

Blume, S. (1980). Clinical research: Casefinding, diagnosis, treatment, and rehabilitation. In *Alcohol and women, Research Monograph No. 1*. Rockville, Md.: National Institute on Alcohol Abuse and Alcoholism.

Kilburg, R. R., Nathan, P. E., & Thoreson, R. W. (Eds.) (1986). *Professionals in distress: Issues, syndromes, and solutions in psychology.* Washington, D.C.: American Psychological Association.

Nathan, P. E. (1982). Psychologists need psychologists, too. APA. *Monitor, 13,* 5.

Nathan, P. E. (1983). Failures in prevention: Why can't we prevent the devastating effect of alcoholism and drug abuse on American productivity? *American Psychologist, 38,* 459–468.

Nathan, P. E. (1984a). Alcoholism prevention in the workplace: Three examples. In P. M. Miller & T. D. Nirenberg (Eds.), *Prevention of alcohol abuse.* New York: Plenum Press.

Nathan, P. E. (1984b). Prevention. In *Fifth Special Report to Congress on Alcohol and Health.* Washington, D.C.: National Institute on Alcohol Abuse and Alcoholism.

Nathan, P. E. (1985). Prevention of alcoholism: A history of failure. In J. C. Rosen & L. J. Solomon (Eds.), *Prevention in health psychology.* Hanover, N.H. & London: University Press of New England.

Nathan, P. E. (1986). Unanswered questions about distressed professionals. In R. R. Kilburg, P. E. Nathan & R. W. Thoreson (Eds.), *Professionals in distress: Issues, syndromes, and solutions in psychology.* Washington, D.C.: American Psychological Association.

Pattison, E. M. (1985). The selection of treatment modalities for the alcoholic patient. In J. H. Mendelson & N. C. Mello (Eds.), *The diagnosis and treatment of alcoholism.* New York: McGraw-Hill.

Thoreson, R. W., Nathan, P. E., Skorina, J. K., & Kilburg, R. R. (1983). The alcoholic psychologist: Issues, problems, and implications for the profession. *Professional Psychology: Research and Practice, 14,* 870–884.

Relevant Biological Factors in the Etiology and Treatment of Alcohol Misuse and Abuse

James W. Smith

For centuries it was simply assumed that those we now call alcoholics drank excessively because they had a moral defect that led them to drink heavily. Later, as psychiatry developed, it was assumed that a deep underlying neurosis or other psychological problem "drove them to drink." As more research results have accumulated, it is becoming clear that alcoholism is neither. It is a genetically influenced biological illness, rather than a character or psychological problem. The first part of this chapter will review the experimental literature that suggests the genetic factors implicated in alcoholism. Then several practical reflections are offered that follow from the genetic basis of alcohol misuse and abuse.

Genetic Factors

The fact that alcoholism tends to run in families has been known since ancient times. Aristotle warned that drunken women "bring forth children like themselves" and Plutarch declared "one drunkard begets another" (Goodwin, 1979). When male or female alcoholics are studied, the rates of alcoholism in their male relatives range from 25 to 50 percent and among their female relatives from 5 to 8 percent (Goodwin, 1979). These rates are at least fivefold what would be expected in the general population.

Twin studies show a much higher concordance for alcoholism in monozygotic (identical) twins (54%) than in dizygotic (fraternal) twins (28%) (Kaij, 1960). The latter show no more concordance for alcoholism than any other sibling. However, the incidence of alcoholism in any sibling of an alcoholic is higher than in the general population (10 percent of drinkers in the United States).

Although the data is limited, there is also information to confirm an increased concordance for alcoholism in monozygotic twins reared apart (Shields, 1962). The reaction of the brain to alcohol also appears to be genetically determined. In twins, high heritability was noted in EEG amplitude and distribution of frequencies. The EEG's of monozygotic twins tended to become still more similar after alcohol (Cropping, 1978).

Adoption studies carried out in Scandinavia (Goodwin et al., 1973) and in the United States (Cadoret, Cain, & Grove, 1980) show that children of alcoholic biologic parents adopted into nonalcoholic families and raised without knowing they have an alcoholic biologic parent were at least four times more likely to develop alcoholism than were comparable adoptees from nonalcoholic biologic parents. In fact, the adopted sons of alcoholic parents did not differ in any significant respect from sons of alcoholics who were not adopted out (Goodwin, Schulsinger, & Moller, 1974).

Confirming information also comes from half sibling studies which show that individuals were more likely to become alcoholic if their biologic parent was alcoholic than if their surrogate parent was alcoholic (Schuckit, Goodwin, & Winokur, 1972).

In a different series of adoption studies in Scandinavia, the interaction of heredity and environment was examined (Cloninger, Bohman, & Sigvardsson, 1981). Two different types of alcoholic families were identified. In one type, alcoholism developed only in the male members. In the other type, it developed in both men and women. The latter variety the investigators termed milieu-limited (or Type I) alcoholism and it accounts for the majority of the cases of alcoholism seen in Sweden. It occurs in both men and women, the symptoms are usually less severe and are associated with "adult onset" alcohol abuse in a biological parent (either father or mother). The alcoholic parent usually has not received treatment for alcoholism and does not have a history of "criminality" (criminality being defined as any kind of legal misconduct that produces official contact with the police).

This type of alcoholism was termed "milieu-limited" because its occurrence and severity is determined by the adoptive home environment. In order for alcoholic symptoms to occur, alcoholism must be present in a biological parent and the adoptive home environment must be "stressful." The home environment most conducive to alcoholism development was "low socioeconomic status" in the adoptive father. If either of these two factors were missing, alcoholism did not develop in the adoptees.

The second type of alcoholism found in these studies was termed "male-limited" (or Type II). As the name suggests, it was found only in men. Sons of alcoholics of this type were nine times more likely to develop alcoholism themselves than were sons of nonalcoholics. This was true regardless of their adoptive home setting.

Male-limited susceptibility was associated with more severe alcoholism symptoms in the biological father (but not the mother). The fathers' alcoholism tended to develop when they were adolescents and they tended to have a record of "criminality."

Biochemical/Constitutional Factors

If one's genetic inheritance may predispose him or her to the development of alcoholism, just what is it that gets inherited? This question has puzzled researchers for many years. A final definitive answer has not yet been reached. However, many interesting pieces of the puzzle have been discovered. A great number of biochemical and other constitutional factors have been investigated. These observations have been carried out in animals (alcohol-preferring versus alcohol-avoiding strains) as well as in humans. Human studies have included active alcoholics and recovered alcoholics as well as nonalcoholics. Studies on high risk but not yet alcoholic groups (e.g., sons of alcoholics), and those of lower risk (e.g., sons of nonalcoholic drinkers) have also been conducted. Some interesting, but not conclusive, differences have been noted.

Animal studies suggest that constitutional factors, probably secondary to genetic variability, may influence the susceptibility to alcoholism. Marked differences in alcohol preference are found between the inbred strains of mice or other animals. Some voluntarily drink large amounts and others avoid it. In fact, there are often substantial differences between the alcohol preference of individual animals from the same litter (Schlesinger, Bennett, & Herbert, 1967). In some cases, certain metabolic differences have been noted between alcohol-preferring and alcohol-avoiding animals (Iida, 1960).

Some of these differences occur not only in alcohol metabolism, but in quantitative and qualitative responses of the brain to alcohol. The differences suggest that alcohol-related genetic and other constitutional differences between humans should also be considered at two levels (in alcohol metabolism and in influence on brain physiology).

In a slightly different area of physiology, tests show that animals experiencing vitamin or certain other deficiency states increase the amount of alcohol they voluntarily consume (Mirone, 1959). Feeding rats cadmium-treated food causes them to voluntarily drink increased amounts of alcohol (*Insight*, 1987). Rats that normally reject alcohol changed so that they preferred alcohol to water after eating the cadmium-laced food. The cadmium may block a stress-reducing neurotransmitter, gamma-aminobutyric acid, and the rats may then attempt to decrease the resulting stress-tension response by self-medicating with the depressant drug, alcohol. This study has implications for humans as well because cadmium contamination of food can occur as a result of fertilization with sewage sludge. Electroplating and battery manufacturing workers are also exposed to dust containing cadmium. In addition, heavy tobacco smokers have elevated blood cadmium levels.

Also, studies producing liver damage by chemical means (e.g., carbon tetrachloride) convert normal nonalcohol-preferring mice into alcohol-drinking mice (Iida, 1960). A somewhat similar phenomenon was reported in humans in which nonalcoholic drinkers of many years standing abruptly turned to an alcoholic drinking pattern following an episode of severe liver damage (e.g., carbon tetra-chloride poisoning or severe viral hepatitis) (O'Hollaren, 1960).

Other alcohol-related physiological differences have also been found in humans. One marked racial difference in response to alcohol is the striking facial flushing and increased pulse pressure observed in the majority of Orientals soon after drinking even small amounts of alcohol. Similar amounts of alcohol ingested by American Caucasians have no noticeable effect (Wolff, 1972). The response is noted as early as the neonatal period and is, therefore, not conditioned by previous use of alcohol. Ewing and colleagues showed that this higher incidence of flushing in persons of Oriental heritage was the result of elevated blood acetaldehyde levels (Ewing, Rouse, & Pellizzari, 1974). Von Wartburg (Von Wartburg et al., 1975) reported that these findings coincide with racial differences of human liver alcohol dehydrogenase, the enzyme that is responsible for the first step in the breakdown of alcohol. The "atypical" enzyme is present in about 85 percent of Orientals and is responsible for producing the higher acetaldehyde levels because it converts alcohol to acetaldehyde more rapidly than the usual variety of the enzyme.

Not only do these Orientals have an alcohol dehydrogenase enzyme that accelerates the formation of acetaldehyde, but about 50 percent of Orientals also lack one of the two liver enzymes that break down acetaldehyde, the enzyme called aldehyde dehydrogenase I. Therefore, they are producing increased amounts of acetaldehyde at the same time they have a slowed removal process resulting in a substantial increase in its accumulation in the blood. This level of accumulation is sufficient to cause symptoms such as flushing, increased heart rate, palpitations, muscle weakness, and stomach discomfort (Goedde & Agarwal, 1986). It is speculated that these somewhat aversive symptoms may explain the low incidence of alcoholism among Orientals. The response is compared to a "mini-antabuse reaction." Antabuse [disulfiram] blocks both the aldehyde dehydrogenase enzymes and leads to a severely uncomfortable acetaldehyde accumulation after alcohol consumption. Indeed, only 2.3 percent of Japanese alcoholics were found to have this aldehyde dehydrogenase deficit while 97.7 percent of the alcoholics had both aldehyde dehydrogenase enzymes intact, just like the majority of Caucasians (Goedde & Agarwal, 1986).

On the other hand, Schuckit and Rayses (1979) found that nonalcoholic male first-degree relatives of alcoholics had a significantly elevated blood acetaldehyde concentration after a dose of alcohol when compared to matched controls. First-degree relatives of alcoholics have a higher (not lower) risk of developing alcoholism, thus casting some doubt on the "mini-antabuse reaction" explanation of the low alcoholism rate among Orientals. However, the level of elevation was mild in these sons of alcoholics compared to the findings in Orientals and may not have been sufficient to cause a great deal of discomfort. This same pattern of elevated post-alcohol acetaldehyde levels is seen in abstinent alcoholics (Korsten et al., 1975), leading to the speculation that it may play a role in the development of the disease of alcoholism.

The elevated acetaldehyde levels may, in some cases, change the state of intoxication, perhaps making it more pleasant (rewarding). This could result from the formation of condensation products with metabolites (breakdown products) of neurotransmitter molecules with the production of addicting, morphine-like alkaloids.

Dopamine is an important neurotransmitter molecule that has received considerable attention. Myers has shown that Dopamine-related condensation products called tetrahydro-isoquinolines (TIQ's), when introduced directly into the brain of rats, will induce a marked increase of voluntary alcohol consumption even in rats that normally reject alcohol. This change in alcohol preference appears to be lifelong since it was noted as long as six months after a single series of infusions

(Myers & Melchior, 1977). In this respect, it resembles the permanent "crossing over the invisible line" that human alcoholics experience (Myers, 1978). Myers proposes that one or all of the TIQ's produced as a result of alcohol consumption act to produce the state of craving for alcohol. The TIQ's are believed to act by way of certain types of opiate receptors in the brain (Myers, 1985).

Another important neurotransmitter, serotonin, also becomes involved in aldehyde-related condensation products called beta-carbolines. Brain injections of beta-carbolines also cause an increase in alcohol consumption, but apparently by a different mechanism. Instead of causing craving like the TIQ's, these compounds are powerful anxiety-inducing drugs. The test animals appear to self-medicate with alcohol which they use as a sedative drug to reduce the stress of anxiety (Myers, 1985). Both types of neurotransmitter condensation products cause animals that normally avoid alcohol to seek out and drink substantial amounts of alcohol—but for different reasons: on the one hand, apparently to make them "feel good"; on the other hand, to reduce their uncomfortable feeling of anxiety.

In other cases differences have been noted in brain chemistry. For example, when brain levels of endorphines (naturally occurring morphine-like compounds) are measured in test animals, there is a very high correlation between the amount of alcohol these animals will voluntarily consume and the endorphine levels. The lowest endorphine-level animals drink the most, the highest drink the least, and the intermediate-level animals drink an intermediate amount (Blum, 1983). These findings may have considerable relevance to alcoholism in humans because we know that the morphine-like molecules called tetrahydroisoquinolines (TIQ's) are formed in the brain as a result of the metabolism of alcohol. These TIQ's may be perceived as much more valuable or rewarding to persons who have naturally low levels. Other people with high endorphine levels may not notice any particular increased feeling of well-being from the TIQ's formed when they drink.

Paralleling these studies in animals, human alcoholics

have been found to have increased TIQ levels (dopamine condensation products) after intoxication (Borg et al., 1980). Brain levels of TIQ's are also found to be elevated at autopsy examination of alcoholics (Sjoquist, Ericksson, & Winblock, 1982). Still other researchers have demonstrated the selective formation of certain beta-carbolines (serotonin condensation products) in the brain following an alcohol challenge (i.e., heavy consumption). In addition, Olsen, Gursey, and Vester (1960) reported that alcoholics demonstrate a defective conversion of the amino acid tryptophan into the neurotransmitter, serotonin—even after prolonged abstinence from alcohol. Recent studies have shown that those individuals with low brain serotonin levels are the individuals most prone to become violent after drinking. They are also the group more likely to attempt suicide by violent means. Alcohol may have a biphasic effect on serotonin metabolism that may relate to a serotonin deficiency model. Alcohol increases serotonin activity during acute intoxication following which serotonin falls to subnormal levels. The "deficient" person would then have two reasons to drink. He or she would first drink to correct the initial deficiency. He or she would later drink to correct the even greater deficiency caused by the byphasic effect of the first drinking (Kent et al., 1985).

Differences have also been found in another area of brain physiology, the brain wave. One particular type of brain wave pattern has received considerable attention. It is the "Event Related Potential" (ERP) labeled P3. Alcoholics have been found to have deficits in the P3 wave (Begleiter, Porjesz, & Tenner, 1980). These deficits were originally believed to be the result of brain damage from alcoholic drinking. However, later studies showed that the same pattern was present in young sons of alcoholics (average age twelve) who had never drunk alcohol. The abnormal patterns were absent in a matched group of sons of nonalcoholics (Begleither et al., 1984), leading the investigators to believe that the brain wave pattern may be a genetically determined antecedent of alcoholism rather than a consequence of brain-damaging heavy drinking. In a series of tests of endocrine and autonomic nervous system functions in drinking alcoholics, abstinent alcoholics (who had no alcohol for two or more years) and nonalcoholic controls, Kissin and his associates (Kissin, Schenker, & Schenker, 1959a, 1959b, 1960; Kissin & Hankoff, 1959) found a series of abnormalities in such areas as adrenal function, regulation of blood pressure, and metabolism of glucose. These differences, they believed, were constitutional characteristics of the alcoholics rather than the effects of alcoholism because the abnormalities were still present more than two years after alcohol intake had been stopped. It might be argued that these changes could be the result of some permanent physiologic derangement produced by heavy alcohol intake over many years in the past. However, even if this is true, the most interesting finding was that the intake of even small doses of alcohol by the alcoholics tended to restore those functions toward normal. That is, the alcoholics tended to be physiologically more normal with alcohol in the system than without alcohol in the system.

Although these and many other similar studies show different pieces to the puzzle, we do not have enough of the pieces in hand to give us the complete picture. Much research work is still needed to show the precise pattern of inheritance of susceptibility for developing the different forms of alcoholism. Even more important, further research is required to determine the best methods for treatment and prevention. Ultimately, prevention is the key to success. No major public health problem has ever been successfully resolved by treatment. Prevention of the disease has always been the winning strategy.

Reflections on the Alcoholism Syndromes

In reflecting on what I have said so far, it is clear that alcoholism is not a matter of weak will power or even a response to neurosis or other underlying psychiatric illness. What we tend to refer to as alcoholism, in the singular, should instead be referred to as "the alcoholisms" in the plural. The alcoholisms are a type of biological (biochemical) disorder in the same sense that diabetes is a biochemical disorder—although a somewhat different type to be sure. What we call diabetes is a collection of symptoms (both physical and psychological), physical signs, and laboratory studies that form a pattern that we call diabetes. One may enter this path in several different ways. One may have a strong family history of the disease and be genetically predisposed. On the other hand, injury or disease may destroy enough of the insulin-producing cells of the pancreas to produce the pattern. In still another way, certain tumors of the adrenal gland may secrete enough of an insulin "neutralizing" hormone to produce still another variety of diabetes. In each case, the person took a different route to the destination we label "diabetes."

We see much the same situation in "the alcoholisms."In each case we have a collection of symptoms (drinking patterns, craving, etc.), physical findings, and laboratory studies that form a pattern that we call "alcoholism." As with diabetes, we know of more than one route that people take to get to that destination (e.g., Cloniger's Type I and Type II alcoholics) and there are suggestions from research of yet other routes that may also exist (e.g., cadmium poisoning).

Nothing that was said above should be taken to imply that environmental factors and psychological factors play no role in alcoholism. Quite the contrary, as Cloninger and colleagues (Cloninger, Bohman & Sigvardsson, 1981, Cloninger & Reich, 1983) noted, a stressful environment was required in addition to a family history of alcoholism in order for Type I alcoholism to become manifest. In other cases, living in an environment that strongly encourages drinking of alcohol almost guarantees that the other types of alcoholism-susceptible individuals will obtain enough alcohol to initiate the process.

The biological nature of "the alcoholisms" also does not preclude attitude or mental states from aggravating the disease. In Alcoholics Anonymous meetings these counterproductive mental states are often referred to as "alcoholic stinking thinking"—a term that is both apt and succinct. However, in the treatment of diabetes physicians see at least as much "diabetic stinking thinking." By that I mean diabetics who refuse to stop eating chocolate cake, who will not take their insulin shots exactly as prescribed, who will not control their weight, and who, in general, contribute as much to their medical deterioration as the alcoholic who persists in drinking. Yet no one would consider saying "in order to be a diabetic you have to have diabetic stinking thinking." Unfortunately, the general public and many professionals are not aware that a similar statement about alcoholism is just as unwarranted. Until that situation is changed alcoholics and their families will continue to get incorrect and possibly dangerous advice. There are several important implications of "the alcoholisms" being biological illnesses, rather than merely a deficiency of discipline or will power.

The first implication is that children or other close blood relatives of alcoholics should be aware of the marked increased risk of developing alcoholism themselves *if they ever start drinking.* For this reason, I strongly recommend that such people never attempt to become social drinkers. The great risk of developing a lethal disease (alcoholism) seems to me to be far too great a price to pay for whatever benefits might be derived from social drinking. Although there are a number of tests that show physiological differences among many alcoholics (e.g., Begleiter's work with EEG's) and even differences in their response to alcohol (e.g., Schuckitt's work with sons of alcoholics), it is too soon to know if those tests will reliably identify those offspring who will become alcoholic if exposed to alcohol. At the very least, we must wait until those individuals who do choose to drink have enough drinking years of experience for the characteristic alcoholism pattern to emerge. Again, this represents a reason to proceed with the utmost caution.

Perhaps the most ominous finding we have so far about young relatives of alcoholics is a recent study by Cloninger and his associates (Cloninger, Reich, & Ligvardsson, 1986). They showed that of those who had at least one first-degree relative who was alcoholic, the probability of developing alcoholism increased markedly in those born more recently. They found that the risk of developing alcoholism by age twenty-five increased by year of birth; from 26 percent risk in those born before 1924, to 34 percent in those born between 1925 and 1934, to 52 percent in those born between 1935 and 1944, to 63 percent in those born between 1945 and 1954, and, finally, to 67 percent in those born after 1954. This extremely high risk level in the last group is all the more striking if one recalls that a significant number of these individuals have not yet passed through the full period of risk. One must also remember that passing the age of twenty-five without signs or symptoms of alcoholism does not confer immunity as a person can become alcoholic at any age.

Unfortunately, most children of alcoholics are still unaware of their risk. In December 1984, the New York State Division of Alcoholism and Alcohol Abuse conducted a telephone survey among 2,000 randomly selected state residents age sixteen and older. The results showed that 16.6 percent of those surveyed indicated that one or both parents were alcoholic. However, only 5 percent of the respondents knew that children of alcoholics were themselves at increased risk. Of particular importance is the fact that the 16.6 percent who had an alcoholic parent were no more likely than the other respondents to be aware of their danger. Moreover, this lack of knowledge may further increase the risk of the development of alcoholism. The children of alcoholics who were unaware of their enhanced risk drank seven times as often and were more likely to drink to intoxication than those who were aware of their risk.

It is clear that, at the very least, the entire population should be made aware of the "genetic risk" of alcoholism. This information should be widely distributed via the various media outlets. It is also important for the information to become a part of the body of knowledge that students acquire from institutions of higher education. In particular, I believe that it should be impossible for a student to graduate from a professional training school without a thorough understanding of alcoholism and chemical dependency in general. This is especially critical when the profession requires dealing with these problems on a frequent basis. These professions include not only the obvious ones—medicine, nursing, psychology, and social work. It is almost as important for graduates of schools of law, police science, and all aspects of business administration to also be well informed on this subject. It is nothing short of bizarre that in approximately 50 percent of medical schools today it is possible to graduate without knowing anything about alcoholism—the third leading killer in the United States. We have also known for many years that a high percentage of business failures and the vast majority of personnel problems are related to alcoholism and other chemical dependencies. As in the case of medical graduates, it is bizarre for accounting and business graduates, in general, to receive no training in this area, an area in which their professional life will require them to work on an almost daily basis. It is obvious that most professionals will need to know much more than the genetic risk factors for alcoholism. A well-rounded curriculum that emphasizes the required chemical dependency knowledge specifically related to each professional discipline would give the students and those they will ultimately serve the best chance for achieving success. By taking some of these educational steps, the university would set an excellent precedent for others and would, at the same time, be instrumental in saving the lives of a number of students and alumni.

References

Begleither, H., Porjesz, B., Bihari, B., & Kissin, B. (1984). Event-related brain potentials in boys at risk for alcoholism. *Science, 225* (4669), 1493–1496.

Begleiter, H., Porjesz, B., & Tenner, M. (1980). Neuroradiological and neurophysiological evidence of brain deficits in chronic alcoholics. *Acta Psychiatrica Scandinavica, 62* (Supplementum 286), 3–13.

Blum, K. (1983). Alcohol and central nervous system peptides. *Substance and Alcohol Actions/Misuse, 4,* 73–87.

Borg, S., Kvande, H., Mognusson, E., & Sjoqvist, V. (1980).

Salsolinol and salsoline in cerebrospinal lumbar fluid of alcoholic patients. *Acta Psychiatrica Scandinavica, 62* (Supplementum 286), 171–177.

Cadoret, R. J., Cain, C. A., & Grove, W. M. (1980). Development in adoptees raised apart from biological relatives. *Archives of General Psychiatry, 37,* 561–563.

Cloninger, C. R., Bohman, M., & Sigvardsson, S. (1981). Inheritance of alcohol abuse: Cross-fostering analysis of adopted men. *Archives of General Psychiatry, 38,* 861–868.

Cloninger, C. R., & Reich, T. (1983). Genetic heterogeneity in alcoholism and sociopathy. In Kety (Ed.), *Genetics of neurological and psychiatric disorders,* pp. 145–166. New York: Raven Press

Cloninger, C. R., Riech, T., Ligvardsson, S., VonKnorring, A. L., & Bohman, M. (1986). The effects of changes in alcohol use between generations on the inheritance of alcohol abuse. In R. Rose (Ed.) *Alcoholism: A medical disorder.* New York: Raven Press.

Cropping, P. (1978). *Pharmacogenetics: Reviews of Physiology, Biochemistry, and Pharmacology, 83,* 12–173.

Ewing, J. A., Rouse, B. A., & Pellizzari, E. D. (1974). Alcohol sensitivity and ethnic background. *American Journal of Psychiatry, 131,* 206–210.

Goedde, H. W., and Agarwal, D. P. (1986). Genetics and alcoholism: Problems and perspectives. In H. W. Goedde and D. P. Agarwal (Eds.) *Progress in clinical and biological research,* Volume 241: *Genetics and alcoholism,* pp. 3–20. New York: Alan R. Liss.

Goodwin, D. W. (1979). Genetic determinants of alcoholism. In J. H. Mendelson and N. K. Mello (Eds.), *The diagnosis and treatment of alcoholism,* p. 59. New York: McGraw-Hill.

Goodwin, D. W., Sculsinger, F., Hermansen, L., Guze, S. B., & Winokur, G. (1973). Alcohol problems in adoptees raised apart from alcoholic biologic parents. *Archives of General Psychiatry, 28,* 238–243.

Goodwin, D. W., Schulsinger, F., Moller, N., et al. (1974). Drinking problems in adopted and nonadopted sons of alcoholics. *Archives of General Psychiatry, 31,* 164–169.

Iida, S. (1960). Experimental studies on the craving for alcohol III: The relationship between alcoholic craving and carbohydrate metabolism. *Japanese Journal of Pharmacology, 10,* 15–20.

Insight. September 7, 1987, p. 55.

Kaij, L. (1960). *Studies on the etiology and sequels of abuse of alcohol.* Department of Psychiatry, University of Lund, Lund, Finland.

Kent, T. A., Campbell, J. L., Pazdernik, T. L., Hunter, R., Gunn, W. H., & Goodwin, D. W. (1985). Blood platelet uptake of serotonin in men alcoholics. *Journal of Studies on Alcohol, 46,* 357–359.

Kissin, B., & Hankoff, L. (1959). The acute effects of ethyl alcohol on the Funkenstein Mecholyl response in male alcoholics. *Journal of Studies on Alcohol, 20,* 696–703.

Kissin, B., Schenker, V., & Schenker, A. C. (1959a). The acute effects of ethyl alcohol and chlorpromazine on certain physiological functions in alcoholics. *Journal of Studies on Alcohol, 20,* 480–492.

Kissin, B., Schenker, V., & Schenker, A. C. (1959b). Adrenal cortical function and liver disease in alcoholics. *American Journal of Medical Science, 238,* 344–353.

Kissin, B., Schenker, V., & Schenker, A. C. (1960). The acute effect of ethanol ingestion on plasma and urinary 17-hydroxycorticoids in alcoholic subjects. *American Journal of Medical Science, 239,* 690–705.

Korsten, M. A., Matsuzaki, S., Feinmna, L., & Lieber, C. S. (1975). High blood acetaldehyde levels after ethanol administration: Difference between alcoholic and nonalcoholic subjects. *New England Journal of Medicine, 292* (8), 386–389.

Mirone, L. (1959). Water and alcohol consumption by mice. *Journal of Studies on Alcohol, 20* (1), 24–27.

Myers, R. D. (1978). Tetrohydroisoquinolines in the brain: The basis of an animal model of alcoholism. *Alcoholism* (NY). 2 (2), 145–154.

Myers, R. D. (1985). Multiple metabolite theory, alcohol drinking and alcogene. In *Aldehyde addicts in alcoholism,* pp. 201–220. New York: Alan R. Liss, Inc.

Myers, R. D., & Melchior, C. L. (1977). Alcoholic drinking: Abnormal intake caused by tetrahydropapaveroline in brain. *Science, 196* (4289), 554–555.

O'Hollaren, P. F. (1960). Differential diagnosis of problem drinkers. *Northwest Medicine, 59,* 639–643.

Olsen, R. E., Gursey, G., & Vester, J. W. (1960). Evidence for a defect in trypotophan metabolism in chronic alcoholism. *New England Journal of Medicine, 263,* 1169–1174.

Schlesinger, K., Bennett, E. L., & Herbert, M. (1967). Effects of genotype and prior consumption of alcohol on rates of ethanol-1-14C metabolism in mice. *Journal of Studies on Alcohol, 28,* 231–235.

Schuckit, M. A., Goodwin, D. W., & Winokur, G. (1972). A study of alcoholism in half siblings. *American Journal of Psychiatry, 128,* 1132–1136.

Schuckit, M. A., & Rayses, V. (1979). Ethanol ingestion differences in blood acetaldehyde concentrations in relatives of alcoholics and controls. *Science, 203* (5), 54–55.

Shields, J. (1962). *Monozygotic twins brought up apart and brought up together.* London: Oxford University Press.

Sjoquist, B. S., Borg, S., & Kvande, H. (1981). Catecholamine derived compounds in urine and cerebrospinal fluid from alcoholics during and after long-standing intoxication. *Substance and Alcohol Actions/Misuse, 2,* 63–72.

Sjoquist, B. S., Fricksson, A., & Winblock, B. (1982). Salsolinol and catecholamines in human brain and their relation to alcohol. *Progress in Clinical and Biological Research, 90,* 57–68.

Von Wartburg, J. P., Berger, D., Rio, M. N., & Rabakoff, P. (1975). Enzymes of biogenic aldehyde metabolism. In M. M. Gross (Ed.) *Alcohol intoxification and withdrawal: Experimental studies, 59,* 119–138. New York: Plenum.

Wolff, P. H. (1972). Ethnic difference in alcohol sensitivity. *Science, 175,* 449–450.

De Loco Magistri
The University's Role in Moral Education

Kevin McDonnell

My title, *De loco magistri* (On the place of the teacher), contrasts with the once widely held justification for the involvement of a college or university in the life of students, the late and unlamented theory that the university acted *in loco parentis*. Those who used this theory did not often reflect on the appropriate role of parents in the life of young adults. Many universities used their *in loco parentis* policies to justify types or levels of control that few parents would impose on their grown children. Having abandoned substitute parenthood as our warrant for university programs or regulations, we need to think anew about justifying our involvement with students' lives.

The issue is hardly new. Socrates was famous in Athens both for his teaching and for his challenge to the claims of the educational and political establishment of his time that it knew how to educate young people. Plato raises the issue in the first lines of his Meno: "Can you tell me, Socrates, whether virtue is acquired by teaching or by practice; or if neither by teaching nor practice, then whether it comes to man by nature, or in what other way?" (Plato in Jowett, 1937). Here is a central question both for Socrates's time and our own—how can virtue be taught?

Before immersing myself in more trouble than even a philosopher deserves, let me clarify a little of what I mean about morality and teaching virtue. The word "morals," like the word "ethics," originally meant mores, customs, or culture. The subject of morality was not moral rules or individual actions, but the good life—how is it good for people to live? When I discuss alcohol use as a moral issue, I do not mean that those with a drinking problem can solve that problem with will power. I also hope that you will not find that I am moralizing, that is, dealing with matters of good and bad in a guilt-producing, preachy way. I think that what and how we drink, and even eat and wear, are important factors in how we live. Therefore, they are part of our morality in the wide sense in which I will use that term.

Even if alcohol education is accepted as part of moral education properly understood, it still needs to be shown that such education is within the province of the university. This chapter will focus, therefore, on the role of the university in moral education, and I will argue that some forms of moral education are proper to the university's educational mission.

Considered in the light of how people live, the question of teaching virtue is as ancient as my opening quotation from Plato's *Meno* suggests. As Alasdair MacIntyre argues in his justly famous book *After Virtue,* the virtues were part of a total cultural context in which Greeks of the fifth century B.C. or Christians of the Middle Ages lived. The concept of the virtues and moral education underwent an enormous shift in the Enlightenment. In its search for the justification of morality, MacIntyre argues, the Enlightenment succeeded in destroying it. By distinguishing the moral from the theological, the legal, and the aesthetic, the Enlightenment destroyed the integrity that a moral culture requires. Moreover, the Enlightenment project was not only the concern of individual thinkers, but became a central occupation of European culture (MacIntyre, 1981).

The Enlightenment substituted individual autonomy for a unified culture as the source of meaning and virtue. By their choices, autonomous individuals are to give meaning to their lives. MacIntyre argues that the breakdown of a shared culture produced by the Enlightenment discovery of the individual leaves us with no common basis for our morality. Both the state of nature and civilization put isolated individuals in competition with each other. Conflict is inevitable. As MacIntyre puts it:

> For each of us is taught to see himself or herself as an
> autonomous moral agent; but each of us also becomes

engaged by modes of practice, aesthetic or bureaucratic, which involve us in manipulative relationships with others. Seeking to protect the autonomy that we have learned to prize, we aspire ourselves not to be manipulated by others; seeking to incarnate our own principles and stand-point in the world of practice, we find no way open to us to do so except by directing towards others those very manipulative modes of relationship which each of us aspires to resist in our own case. (MacIntyre, 1981, 66)

On MacIntyre's account, therefore, moral education is either impossible because it interferes with autonomy, or it rests on bad faith because it both espouses and betrays autonomy.

Pluralism is the cultural expression of the autonomous individual. Except for autonomy and pluralism, all other values are thought relative to the individuals or subcultures which hold them. Allan Bloom (1987) in his recent book, *The Closing of the American Mind*, exploits the concern of many educated Americans that something is astray in our educational system. Increasing relativism among students indicates that colleges are not "turning out the kind of people" we would like our offspring to become.

The history of American higher education provides striking confirmation of MacIntyre's thesis. Although the Enlightenment was a project of the eighteenth century, its effects were not felt in higher education until the end of the nineteenth. Woodrow Wilson, writing in 1896, still speaks of a tradition in which it was a university's claim of distinction to have formed people in a certain moral character:

> Princeton sent upon the public stage an extraordinary number of men of notable quality in those days; became herself for a time in some visible sort the academic center of the Revolution, fitted, among the rest, the man in whom the country was to recognize the chief author of the Federal Constitution.

> Princetonians are never tired of telling how many
> public men graduated from Princeton in Wither-
> spoon's time,—twenty Senators, twenty-three
> Representatives, thirteen Governors, three Judges
> of the Supreme Court of the Union; one Vice-Pres-
> ident and a President; all within a space of twenty
> years, and from a college which seldom had more
> than a hundred students. . . . What takes our admir-
> ation and engages our fancy in looking back to that
> time is the generous union then established in the
> college between the life of philosophy and the life
> of the state. (Wilson, reprinted in Hofstadter &
> Smith, 1961, 686)

There is a record of which even Socrates would be proud.

Before Wilson wrote these words, however, American higher education had already changed enormously. The colleges of revolutionary times had developed into universities. Charles William Eliot, president of Harvard from 1869, expanded the elective system of curriculum construction and defended it as crucial to the development of universities. He argued that a university must give its students freedom in choosing their course of studies, the opportunity to pursue specialized studies, and a discipline which makes each individual responsible for his or her own conduct. He attacked the isolation which characterized many colleges and suggested that schools be located in major centers of culture. Students must find moral guidance within themselves; they cannot rely on the university to provide it. He concludes: "It is a distinct advantage of the genuine university method that it does not pretend to maintain any paternal or monastic discipline over its students, but frankly tells them that they must govern themselves" (Eliot, reprinted in Hofstadter & Smith, 1961, 714).

The history of American higher education shows that Harvard has won out over Princeton. The university model dominates our thinking about higher education and, as Eliot's remarks make clear, that model separates the intellectual from the moral spheres of education. Students are only students in the classroom; outside that context they are autonomous individuals.

When, therefore, society wants to foster moral values, as it does when we want to improve the character of medical care, the standards of lawyers, or the ethics of business leaders, the contemporary university is at something of a loss. In order to fit the curriculum, these concerns must be translated into courses. Universities must hire expert professors to teach these courses, yet often these experts are recruited from philosophy or theology rather than from the discipline, for example law or medicine, most directly involved. Should universities require such courses? Are they at the core of professional education or are they peripheral? How can they be taught without indoctrination and while recognizing the plurality of answers to difficult moral questions that characterizes our society? The discussion of courses in professional ethics raises exactly the challenges to the principle of autonomy that MacIntyre described.

My argument here is that alcohol education should be seen as part of the education of character. Character education, however, challenges some of our basic assumptions about the university because it undermines the hard distinction between facts and values which has been a dogma of American higher education since the turn of this century.

Almost as an aside, let me say that there is no issue here about alcohol treatment programs which, as part of a comprehensive health services plan, serve the needs of individual students and faculty and staff where their participation is included. So long as they are part of health services, however, such efforts will be peripheral to the controlling purposes of the university. Alcohol treatment programs will be seen as medical care and therefore as preconditions for education rather than part of the university's proper mission.

I will discuss three ways of dealing with character education in the contemporary university. The first suggestion, and in some ways the most plausible, is to give it up. One can accept President Eliot's picture of the role of the university and MacIntyre's analysis of our culture's disintegration, thus leaving ourselves to our private interests and hoping that others will leave us alone. The second possibility is to model character education on professional education and introduce value courses in all areas of the curriculum much as we have introduced medical ethics and business ethics into our professional curricula. Finally, we will consider the revivification of general education and its potential for character formation.

Alasdair MacIntyre believes that we no longer have the intellectual wherewithal to act as a culture. While he readily admits that fragments of earlier cultures survive and some strong subcultures persist, none of these can enter public debate without being dismissed as sectarian. They are pushed toward "the pluralism which threatens to submerge us all." Within a pluralistic society, he argues, there is no common moral culture, and attempts at moral education are doomed.

"What matters at this stage," MacIntyre argues, "is the construction of local forms of community within which civility and the intellectual and moral life can be sustained through the new dark ages which are already upon us" (1981, 210). There is simply no way of reconstructing the moral communities that used to make the good life possible. For all his wonderful talk of ancient Athens, MacIntyre knows that we cannot live in the past nor rush the future into birth. Therefore he recommends that, like the monks of the sixth century, we take to mountain fastnesses, fortresses of civility and culture, and await a new moral unity which will allow us to live together again.

Despite my agreement with much of what MacIntyre says about the culture of autonomy, however, I find his account of modern moral life unpersuasive. There is chaos, but there has always been chaos. There may be more disagreement than there was in previous eras, but that is hard to say because our culture urges us to look for disagreement. Agreement is hard for us to handle. We often think it the result of some conspiracy. Academics, in particular, thrive on disagreement. Much of MacIntyre's pessimism seems to spring from his thinking and talking almost entirely within the culture of a few important universities. Much the same criticism can be made of Allan Bloom. Both men seem strangers to the moral worlds of medicine, law, and government. MacIntyre is so imbued with his own story of intellectual history that he sometimes speaks as though we are just puppets in the hands of some conceptual scheme (cf. MacIntyre, 1981, 244–245).

Most of us and most of our students find ourselves within a complex of coherent moral communities—family, church, school, etc. Within these communities we recognize common problems from alcoholism to plagiarism, and we even have some wisdom about handling them. MacIntyre's funeral oration for civility and morality is premature.

A second possibility is to add character education, alcohol education included, to the university curriculum on the model of our programs in professional ethics. While this is one way to get students and faculty to take it seriously, it is very doubtful that standard academic structures are very helpful to moral development. Here I am reflecting on my own experience in teaching medical ethics. Future physicians and nurses should understand the moral presuppositions of their work, and they need to master the tools of moral argument so they can make themselves understood in the wider intellectual and moral community.

Much of the material presented in a standard medical ethics course, however, does not emerge from the medical community in which the problems arise, but from philosophers approaching medicine as merely an application of general moral principles. In their efforts to carry out the Enlightenment project of rationalizing morality, philosophers extend their own activity rather than entering into the work of other professionals. To make medical ethics professionally respectable, we have built up a substantial body of literature, much of it quite remote from the actual concerns of nurses, physicians, or patients. Only by building such a literature can we assure ourselves that we are really "doing philosophy."

An academic discipline, therefore, can function as a Procrustean bed on which moral development and moral education can be chopped to size. The standard university course does not provide an effective format for moral instruction. In the Hastings Center study of ethics teaching, for example, Daniel Callahan (1980) argues that:

> The whole point of an ethics course would seem to be that of inquiring into what should count as good behavior. The purpose of an ethics course—that of critical inquiry—would be begged by a preestablished blueprint of what will count as acceptable moral behavior. (69-70)

When Callahan talks about "the whole point" and "the purpose," what he has in mind is exactly the Enlightenment project of critical inquiry. In making these remarks, moreover, he neglects his own warning that moral assertions, in fact all assertions, depend upon some assumptions (cf. Callahan, 1980, p. 63). Issues of medical ethics arise because patients and their caregivers wrestle with sometimes conflicting ideals of appropriate care. Any examination of good medical practice counts on such ideals. As presented in the classroom, medical ethics is a severely limited enterprise. To be effective, I believe, these courses must be integrated with clinical experience. While classroom discussion of issues is helpful, even such helpfulness can lead to the deception that the university is effective within the confines of its current methods.

Alcohol education would not profit by becoming part of a standard academic course. Beware, however, the great engine of academia. It can take almost anything and shape it to university methods. It would be unwise for alcohol education to go the way of such other forms of moral education as medical or legal ethics. Since the standard academic structure is so modestly successful in these areas, it is unlikely to be more successful outside those limits of professional education which give these courses some power.

James Smith is correct, I believe, in remarking that professionals should not complete their training without knowing how alcohol use affects their professions and what, as professionals, they should be prepared to do about alcohol misuse. I believe, however, that this kind of education is not effective until young professionals have begun their work. Not only physicians, but lawyers, accountants, and teachers must confront alcohol issues. Unfortunately, most apprenticeships (residency, practice teaching) are so focused on technical matters that there is little consideration of issues of ethics and character.

Having, I hope, persuaded you to turn away from both MacIntyre's despair and Callahan's standard university structures, let me present a very ordinary view of the proper role of the teacher. The role of the teacher is to teach. In contemporary academic practice, this answer is not as ordinary as it sounds. In schools both large and small, professors devote increasing time to research.

This is not the place to advocate specific changes in curriculum or faculty activity. I will, however, share some speculation about what might happen if faculty began to take teaching more seriously. To begin with, we might rethink general education, core courses, the liberal arts, or whatever one calls the subjects outside the major field and covered during the first two years of baccalaureate study. (I will refer to these courses as "general education.") Adler and Hutchins at Chicago and Conant at Harvard, along with many others, vigorously discussed general education in the 1940s and 1950s. We moved away from this debate in the 1960s. After student political involvement subsided, the debate about general education seemed to fade away. Departments now structure general education requirements to ensure that students have certain prerequisite courses. As departments, they do not concern themselves about what educated people should know.

The debate on general education has now resumed, although neither Hirsch nor Bloom seem to have the stature of those who previously carried on the argument. I believe, however, that it is more important to carry on the discussion than to arrive at a definitive solution. If faculty think about their teaching, they will soon generate many proposals about good teaching. They will probably even publish some of them, challenging the more traditional research in their fields, and provoking other scholar-teachers to respond.

A reform in general education will also change the relation between students and faculty. It might force us to take students seriously again. "Scholarly productivity," apparently so much easier to quantify than teaching, has become the primary measure of faculty success in universities and the "leading" colleges. As the recent debate at Stanford seems to illustrate, thinking about what undergraduates should learn makes us view our own disciplines in a broader way than we need to do when we are doing research. We also will force each other to answer questions about the value of what we are doing, questions usually suppressed by the specialization scholarship requires.

Taking teaching seriously also demands that we think about how we teach. One cannot teach Plato's dialogues without realizing that they demand a response from the reader. Laying out the arguments of the dialogue to a large audience violates their structure. One cannot read Freud's discussion of a patient's psychic processes without becoming more conscious of one's own. The sheer size of most schools is an obstacle to the kind of teaching that almost any general education proposal demands. Since it does not seem that schools will decrease in size, they will have to reorganize themselves internally, as several have done, to provide students with the contact with professors and each other which their studies require.

America is engaged in a great effort in mass higher education. One reason that I am using the term "general education" rather than "liberal arts" is that part of the original meaning of "liberal" referred to those people who were free to pursue a life of learning because they did not have to work. I take it to be a blessing that most of our students are preparing for a profession. We have a responsibility to show them, however, that their work can be placed in the context of a good life. They need the discipline of learning both to stay with their professions and also to pursue the concerns of whole human beings.

Questions about general education inevitably raise questions of value. As it certainly has at Stanford, debating general education might shatter some of the yawning calm that settled over our campuses in the 1980s. Not only will renewed debate challenge faculty, but faculty will begin to rediscover that general education has an intrinsic morality. Moral formation does not have to be added to liberal learning because it is already present both in structure and content.

There is, for example, a morality that is intrinsic to being a good scientist. Good scientists do not fudge their data; they publish the full results of their experiments in ways to make them replicable. They are not defensive about their discoveries, but look to see them overturned by later developments. As the history of science shows, these moral qualities are ideals more than the realities of daily life in the sciences, but they are nevertheless inherent in any scientific endeavor.

Similar remarks can be made about the humanities. Whatever one's approach to literature or history, that approach is shaped by and shapes one's values and view of the world. Neutrality and objectivity are themselves ideals. Reading literature or studying history introduces stories of the guilty and the great. Teaching these stories forces us to think concretely about the good life.

While it is a commonplace, and a truth, that we will die as teachers without research, it is also true that we will die as scholars without teaching. (There are, of course, exceptions to both these generalizations.) If the intellectual life is addressed only to a narrow group of professional scholars, we will betray the driving force of scholarship. Philosophy, for example, has confined itself to an incredible scholasticism and has lost touch with any audience beyond professional philosophers. The same can be said of many of the humanities and even the arts.

What has all this to do with alcohol education? Please do not take me to be saying that the reform of general education will cure individuals of their dependence on alcohol. We teachers, however, do have a role in the lives of our students. We should not stand in the place of parents, or government, or courts. We are not counselors or physicians. We do not need to stand in the place of others. We should stand in our own place; we are teachers. If we take up our role as teachers, things may begin to change on campus. Only the faculty can move the intellectual life, an important facet of the good life, back to a central position on campus. In doing so we may recapture our own disciplines, and perhaps even find some disciples.

References

Bloom, A. (1987). *The closing of the American mind*. New York: Simon and Schuster.

Callahan, D. (1980). Goals in the teaching of ethics. In D. Callahan & S. Bok (Eds.), *Ethics teaching in higher education*. New York: Plenum Press.

Eliot, C. W. (1961). Liberty in education. Reprinted in Hofstadter and Smith (Eds.), *American higher education: A documentary history* (Vol. II). Chicago: University of Chicago Press.

Jowett, B. (Translator) (1937). *The dialogues of Plato*. New York: Random House.

MacIntyre, A. (1981). *After virtue*. Notre Dame, Ind.: University of Notre Dame Press.

Wilson, W. (1961). Princeton in the Nation's Service. Reprinted in Hofstadter and Smith (Eds.), *American higher education: A documentary history*. Chicago: University of Chicago Press.

PART II

CHARACTERISTICS OF
EFFECTIVE HELPING PROGRAMS

Motivating Young Adults for Treatment and Lifestyle Change

William R. Miller and Victoria C. Sanchez

A central concern in the psychology of motivation is how to get people to do something they are disinclined to do, even though you think they should. The usual situation is that Person *A* perceives a problem in Person *B*, conceives of a solution to the problem, and sets out to persuade Person *B* to undertake that solution. The perceived solution may be formal treatment of some kind, or it may be a change in behavior and lifestyle.

Some conceptions of motivation understand it as a trait, or at least a relatively inertial state consistent across situations. In this view, level of motivation (as trait or state) can be measured as a characteristic of the individual. The person is presumed to carry this level of motivation with him or her into each new situation. With this static understanding of motivation often comes the notion that there is relatively little one can do to help someone change until the person "is ready," "hits bottom," or "is sufficiently motivated."

Stages of Change

More recent models of motivation, however, construe it as a more malleable process. Prochaska and DiClemente (1986) have proposed a transtheoretical model based on studies of people who have made significant changes without the help of formal treatment. Their model suggests that change occurs in predictable stages, of which the first four are of interest for present purposes.

The first stage is *precontemplation*, at which point the person is not even considering the prospect of change. In this stage, the individual is unlikely to perceive a need for change. If it is suggested that she or he has a problem, the reaction may be more one of surprise than of defensiveness. In precontemplation, by definition, it is someone else who perceives the problem. Needless to say, precontemplators rarely come seeking help.

In the *contemplation* stage, the person is more ambivalent. His or her motivations are a mixture of vectors favoring and resisting change. One analogy for this stage is a seesaw, one side of which favors change while the other favors status quo. Figure 1 shows such a contemplation seesaw with regard to drinking behavior. On the "change" side of the seesaw are the perceived negative effects of drinking and the potential benefits of change. On the other side are the perceived positive benefits of drinking and the feared or actual negative consequences of making a change in drinking. Allowed to talk freely, a contemplator will discuss both sides of the seesaw. Confronted with arguments on behalf of one side ("You're an alcoholic, and you have to quit drinking"), however, the contemplator is likely to respond by defending the opposite side (Miller, 1983).

CONTEMPLATION
Cost–Benefit Balance

Negative Effects of Drinking
Positive Benefits of Sobriety

Negative Effects of Sobriety
Positive Benefits of Drinking

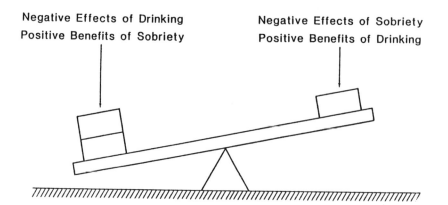

In theory, at least, the seesaw tips more heavily toward change at some point. This may occur gradually over time, or may happen in response to a sudden shock or a crisis. At this point of *determination* the person's talk has a different sound. Less ambivalent, the person acknowledges a problem in need of change and seeks alternative solutions. "I've got to do something about this. It's serious! What can I do?" At this decisional point the person requires no further motivational boosting, but rather needs help in choosing the best alternatives for action. The determination point, we believe, is a window of opportunity that is open for a finite period of time. A person in determination should be helped immediately, not put on hold or on a waiting list. If the period of determination passes and the window closes, the person returns to contemplation, and an opportunity for change has been lost.

Ideally, the person chooses a change strategy and moves on to the next stage of action: implementing the plan. In studying the change process, Prochaska and DiClemente have found that the contemplation and action stages tend to blend into one another, and that the moment of determination is difficult to capture. As a person's contemplation balance begins to tip toward change, he or she may begin to consider and try out actions to implement change. The remaining two stages in the transtheoretical model are *maintenance* (sustaining changes accomplished by action) and *relapse* (reverting, at least temporarily, to the previous pattern). Should relapse occur, the person must in effect go around the circle again through contemplation, determination, and action.

In this model, then, motivation is not a trait, but rather a process. At any point in time, an individual can be understood as being somewhere in this cycle of stages of change. What is needed to help the person progress toward change will vary, depending upon her or his present stage. At *precontemplation* the person needs increased awareness of the risk involved in his or her present pattern. In *contemplation* the process is one of removing weights from one side of the balance and adding them to the other, favoring change. In *determination* the person may need assistance in selecting an optimal strategy for change, and in *action* the likely need is for help in carrying out the plan.

Table 1
Counselor's Role and Suggested Therapeutic Process
at Various Stages of Change Process

Stage of Change	Counselor's Role	Process
Precontemplation	Create perception of risk	Feedback
Contemplation	Elicit personal concerns and perceived need for change	Motivational interviewing
Determination	Negotiate alternatives	Matching
Action	Assist person in changing	Referral, Treatment
Maintenance	Assist person in maintaining changes	Relapse prevention
Relapse	Assist person in resuming change strategies	Same as above

Locus of Motivation

Another important shift in thinking during recent years has been the realization that motivation is not simply a characteristic of the individual, but rather the product of interpersonal exchanges. Any sales enterprise is predicated on this assumption—that motivation (in this case, to buy) is at best only partially present in the individual. The adept salesperson does not wait for motivated customers to come along, but instead practices a set of transactional skills designed to increase motivation to buy. A sale is the result of an interpersonal interaction and is very much affected by the skills of the salesperson.

Ample evidence suggests that this is also true in the arena of treatment for addictive behaviors. The pretreatment characteristics of individuals often turn out to be inconsistent and relatively poor predictors of change. Actions such as entering treatment, persisting or dropping out, and complying with an intervention plan appear to be highly influenced by aspects of the environment and by the skills and attributes of therapists (Miller, 1985). Given this picture, it is not meaningful to ask, "How motivated is this person?" without reference to a particular strategy or situation. Rather, motivation is highly influenced by situations and by the people with whom one interacts. This means that motivation is better understood as a characteristic of *environments* and *relationships* than as a trait of individuals.

Consider the following experiment (Miller, Benefield, & Tonigan, 1993). We advertised to a metropolitan community the availability of a free "Drinker's Check-up," designed to help people determine whether they are being harmed by their drinking. Those who expressed interest in a check-up were screened, then given three hours of assessment designed to detect risk factors and the harmful effects of overdrinking on neuropsychological, physical, social, and psychological dimensions (Miller, Sovereign, & Krege, 1988). Virtually all of those who sought a check-up showed evidence of serious problems related to their drinking.

One week later they returned for feedback of their results. It was at this point that participants were randomized to receive one of two different styles of feedback. Both groups were given the true results of their tests, but the counselor's style was varied. One style was directive and confrontational. The client was given the label "alcoholic" (when justifiable), and was strongly advised to change his or her drinking. If the person protested that the problem wasn't that serious, the counselor confronted her or him with evidence from the check-up, and repeated the advice. The other style was client-centered, presenting the feedback and then eliciting and reflecting the person's own reactions to it (Miller, 1983). The counselor's style during this single hour of feedback was the only difference between groups.

There were immediate differences in what happened during counseling. Those in the directive condition showed much more of what would be called "resistance" or "denial." Verbal responses coded from tapes of these sessions revealed that clients in the directive condition showed more arguing, interrupting, denial of problems, and passive following. Those randomly assigned to client-centered feedback, on the other hand, were more likely to be expressing concerns about their problems and acknowledging a need for change. That is, the motivation, resistance, and denial levels of these problem drinkers were determined by what the *therapist* did during counseling.

Does this have anything to do with actual changes in behavior? We conducted follow-ups with these people eighteen months later to determine whether they had changed. The sharp reductions in drinking that we saw in both groups at six weeks were maintained a year and a half later. Next we examined the relationship between what happened in the feedback session and drinking behavior eighteen months later. There was a strong relationship between counselor style and drinking. The more the counselor had confronted, the more the client was drinking at eighteen months. The more the counselor had listened and been supportive (consistent with the client-centered style), the less the person was drinking a year and a half later. Long-term drinking was similarly predictable from the client's level of resistance during the feedback session: the more resistance and denial shown, the more he or she was drinking eighteen months later. Either therapist or client behavior during the session accounted for over 40 percent of the variance in long-term drinking outcome. Had this not been an experiment, one might conclude that clients who are resistant and "in denial" evoke less support from therapists, and are less likely to change. Recall, however, that client resistance was strongly influenced by the randomly assigned therapist style. Both the amount of resistance shown and the magnitude of change in drinking were predictable from aspects of how the counselor interacted with the client.

This study suggests that, while some of the behaviors we call "resistance" may indeed be predictive of outcome, we need to think about resistance (and its semantic opposite, motivation) in a new way. Motivation and resistance appear to be susceptible to influence, even from brief interventions, and in turn to impact important behavior outcomes.

FRAMES: Critical Elements of Change

The Drinker's Check-up findings discussed above are not isolated results. Studies conducted in at least fourteen nations now indicate that relatively brief interventions can have a lasting impact upon problem drinking, and may be comparable in effect to more extensive treatments (for reviews see Holder et al., 1991; Institute of Medicine, 1990). A comparison of those brief interventions which have shown significant impact suggested to us several common elements that may represent important factors in inducing motivation for change. They can be summarized in the acronym FRAMES.

One common element appears to be personal *Feedback* regarding risk status. Most of the brief interventions studied thus far have included a substantial preintervention assessment which provided each individual with more or less formal feedback about the extent of alcohol-related problems. The advice intervention in the famous Edwards et al. (1977) study, for example, was preceded by three hours of comprehensive evaluation. Assessment feedback is the foundation of our Drinker's Check-up intervention. Such feedback is personalized, and should not be confused with education about the detrimental effects of alcohol on people in general. Alcohol education of the latter kind has generally been found to have little or no impact upon drinking and related problems in either prevention or treatment applications. Personal feedback, in contrast, is a consistent theme in effective motivational programs (Miller, 1985).

Most of the impactful brief interventions have also emphasized, either directly or implicitly, the individual's personal *Responsibility* for change. A common form is the statement that it is up to the individual to alter his or her own drinking, and that in reality no one else can do this for him or her. It is the polar opposite of turning oneself over to a treatment agent or program to be changed. This is consistent with a larger literature in social psychology emphasizing the importance of internal attribution (Kopel & Arkowitz, 1975) and intrinsic motivation (Deci, 1975).

Brief direct *Advice* to change has been associated with reductions in addictive behaviors (Burnum, 1984). An example is unambiguous advice from one's primary care physician to stop smoking (Russell et al., 1979) or drinking (Elvy, Wells, & Baird, 1988). Although the overall success rates from simple advice may be low, clear admonishment appears to be an important component in increasing motivation for lifestyle change.

Motivation also seems to be enhanced when one can freely choose a change strategy from a *Menu* of alternatives, rather than being given only a single option. Providing a variety of possible approaches increases the opportunity for effective client-treatment matching (Miller & Hester, 1986), and may also enhance the important perception of personal choice and control which promotes intrinsic motivation (Deci, 1975). Self-help instructional programs often offer a menu of alternative change strategies, from which readers can select appropriate methods for their own situation (Miller & Muñoz, 1982; Robertson et al., 1986). The menu approach can apply not only to strategies but also to goals of change. Although treatment interventions with alcoholics have traditionally insisted on lifelong abstinence as the only acceptable goal, this approach is likely to be unacceptable to many young people whose drinking has not yet caused substantial harm. Prevention and early intervention programs are more likely to attract young people and motivate change if they are responsive to individual differences in goals for change (Miller, 1987).

The elements discussed here necessarily interact with the therapeutic style of the intervention agent. What style is most effective in motivating change? Studies of therapists working with problem drinkers are consistent in pointing to therapist empathy as a strong predictor of success (Ends & Page, 1957; Miller, Taylor, & West, 1980; Miller, Benefield, & Tonigan, 1993; Milmoe et al.,

1967; Valle, 1981) and clinical descriptions of effective brief interventions have often included explicit mention of *Empathy* as a key element of style (e.g., Chafetz, 1961; Edwards et al., 1977). The kind of empathy meant here is not that of having had similar experiences (e.g., being a recovering alcoholic), but rather the therapeutic skill operationally defined by Carl Rogers and his students (Truax & Carkhuff, 1967). This empathic process of reflective listening and accurate understanding appears to be one of the stronger markers of therapist effectiveness with problem drinkers.

Finally, *Self-efficacy* emerges as a common theme in programs which motivate change. Not to be confused with self-esteem, self-efficacy is the belief in one's ability to perform a specific task or accomplish a specific change (Bandura, 1982). The message, "You can do it!" has often been explicitly or implicitly included in effective brief interventions. A therapist's own belief in the client's ability to change has been found to manifest itself as a self-fulfilling prophecy with alcoholics (Leake & King, 1977). Such optimism that change is possible appears to be an important asset in accomplishing it.

No one element among these six (Feedback, Responsibility, Advice, Menu, Empathy, and Self-efficacy) may be necessary or sufficient to tip the contemplation balance. Interventions, even brief, which have yielded larger effects on drinking problems have included different combinations of these elements.

Protection Motivation Theory

What are the motivational processes underlying these change strategies? A useful organizing model is Rogers's *protection motivation theory* (Rogers, 1975; Rogers, Deckner, & Mewborn, 1978; Rogers & Mewborn, 1976). It is, in essence, a health beliefs model, emphasizing the importance of cognitive-perceptual processes in determining whether or not an individual will engage in a health-related behavior. Quite applicable to drinking and other drug use, it can also be used to study a wide variety of other behaviors such as dental hygiene practices, wearing of a seat belt or protective clothing, safe sex practices, and medication compliance.

One key element of the model is the perceived level of risk—the level of health threat as judged by the individual. This is influenced by two factors: perceived *probability* of risk (How likely is it to happen to me?), and perceived *seriousness* of risk (If it did happen to me, how bad would it be?). These two factors interact, perhaps in multiplicative fashion, to determine the overall level of perceived risk severity and are depicted in Figure 2. Without a threshold level of such concern, there is insufficient motivation for change. A high level of perceived risk engenders a search for possible actions that one could take to reduce risk, and also yields emotional arousal.

Yet the mere arousal of fear or anxiety does not reliably lead to behavior change. The literature on fear induction (sometimes pejoratively called "scare tactics") is mixed, with some successes and some failures (Miller, 1985). Rogers proposes that a second variable influences whether or not perceived risk will yield a change in behavior. This second factor is self-efficacy. Once the search for possible actions is underway, the outcome depends upon whether or not the person identifies at least one strategy which is (1) perceived to be acceptable and possible to use, and (2) perceived to be likely to help, to effectively reduce risk. If such an alternative is found, the person is more likely to engage in risk reduction behavior. If anxiety is aroused but no efficacious solution is identified, the individual instead engages in fear reduction to diminish emotional discomfort. The latter resembles the classic "defense mechanisms" such as denial, rationalization, and projection.

Within this conceptual system, motivation for change would be effectively increased by interventions which enhance these two factors: perceived risk and self-efficacy. The elements of the FRAMES approach identified above fit this general description. Personal feedback and clear advice to change are aimed at increasing the person's perception of risk. Our Drinker's Check-up data further suggest that an empathic style increases the client's acceptance of risk perceptions, whereas a confron-

Figure 2. Protection Motivation Theory (Rogers)

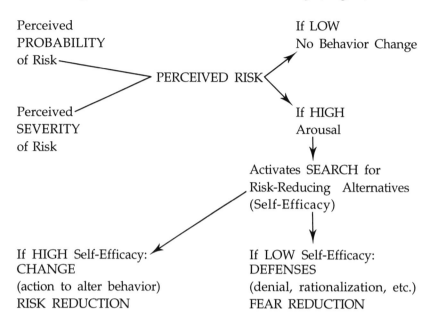

tational style tends to evoke resistance and diminish risk perception (cf. Miller, 1983). The second factor, self-efficacy, is itself one of the six components of FRAMES. The perception of self-efficacy may be further enhanced by an emphasis on personal responsibility, and by offering a menu from which to choose personally acceptable and useful strategies.

Models of Etiology

Application of the motivational principles and findings described above requires an examination of more general models of the nature and causes of alcohol problems. No intervention program is developed or implemented without an implicit model of the etiology of the problems to be addressed.

Although there are many viable alternative models of the etiology of alcohol problems, U.S. prevention and intervention programs have been guided largely by a single conceptual approach which might be termed the American disease model (Miller & Hester, 1989). Briefly stated, this model asserts that certain individuals (alcoholics) are constitutionally and qualitatively different from normal people, and are thereby rendered uniquely vulnerable to alcohol and incapable of controlling their consumption of it. This unique vulnerability is understood to be irreversible, and lifelong abstinence is seen as the only possible route to recovery (Alcoholics Anonymous, 1976). The implications of this model for prevention are clear but limited: it is essential to identify those who have this unique susceptibility and persuade them not to drink.

This model served as a useful transition in the United States during the middle decades of this century. Prior models had either stressed the personal responsibility of the individual for drinking and its consequences (moral model) or construed alcohol as a drug so dangerous that no one could use it in moderation (prohibition). After the repeal of prohibition in 1933, neither of these models was fully satisfactory. The American disease model proposed that only *certain* individuals were incapable of handling alcohol. The unspoken implication is that other (nonalcoholic) individuals can use alcohol with relative impunity. This proved beneficial to large elements of U.S. society. For alcoholics, it diminished the moral blame of the prior era, construing them as sick rather than sinful. For other drinkers, it offered the illusion that only alcoholics are at risk, and thus that others could drink without worry. (This also set the stage for struggles about who is and is not alcoholic.) The medical profession embraced a disease conception of alcoholism, implying it to be a condition properly treated by the medical profession. The liquor industry, too, has been enthusiastic in its support of this view of alcohol problems, which exonerates alcohol of causal responsibility. Alcoholism, in this view, is not caused by alcohol, but rather by a constitutional abnormality found in a small minority of individuals.

It has been hotly debated whether this etiologic model accurately describes a particular subpopulation of alcoholics (e.g.,

Heather & Robertson, 1983). What experts from Jellinek (1960) to Cahalan (1987) have recognized, however, is that regardless of the truth and applicability of the American disease model for a subgroup, it fails to account for a very substantial proportion of our society's problems related to alcohol (cf. Institute of Medicine, 1990; Moore & Gerstein, 1981).

One unfortunate effect of the American disease model has been the implication that there are only two kinds of people in the world: those who cannot control their drinking (alcoholics), and those who can drink safely. Acceptance of this assumption can lead to the idea that unless one is an alcoholic there is no reason to be concerned about drinking. Jellinek, in his classic treatise on *The Disease Concept of Alcoholism* (1960), explicitly warned that an overextension of the American disease conception of alcoholism would undermine societal sanctions against intoxication. That is, if a society accepts the unique susceptibility view as the total truth about alcoholism, it tends to become careless in its control of alcohol, drinking, and intoxication. In seeking to escape from a moral blame of alcoholics, society seems to have forgotten what was so emphasized during the temperance era—that alcohol is a very dangerous drug.

Debates continue to rage in the courts and in the press as to whether or not alcoholism "is a disease" (e.g., Fingarette, 1988). The subject of these debates, however, is actually whether alcoholism is the particular kind of disease described by the American disease model. Progress might be promoted by acknowledging that there are disease-like properties to alcohol problems (few would contest this), and seeking to discern what kind (or kinds) of disease we might be facing. Relatively few of the maladies addressed by modern medicine resemble the black-and-white dichotomy proposed by the American disease model of alcoholism. Rather, many of the chronic diseases which are the major killers of our day come in shades of grey and are intimately involved with lifestyle and environmental factors.

A public health model offers a promising conceptual compromise for understanding alcohol problems as a complex disease process (Miller & Hester, 1989). The public health approach emphasizes three types of etiologic factors in the understanding of disease processes: agent, host, and environment. The *agent*, often a microorganism, in this case is a drug—ethyl alcohol. The agent in itself contains destructive propensities. Some agents (e.g., the AIDS retrovirus) are more consistently and devastatingly destructive than others. It was the agent factor (alcohol) which was so strongly emphasized during the prohibition era. In an exclusively agent view, alcoholism is caused by alcohol.

For most diseases, however, there are substantial individual differences in susceptibility of the *host*. Here a variety of factors come into consideration: heredity, biochemistry, physiology, and lifestyle. The moral, psychodynamic, and American disease models all place heavy emphasis on host factors, to the exclusion of others. In an exclusively host view, alcoholism is caused by constitutional (or lifestyle) factors.

The third etiologic component of a public health model is the *environment*. Many diseases are spread by exposure to certain environmental risk conditions. Sociocultural views of alcohol problems emphasize factors such as the availability of alcohol, social sanctions against intoxication, and peer pressure or role models. Certain environments and societies impose a substantially higher risk of alcohol problems. Alcoholism, in this view, is responsive to aspects of the environment.

The wisdom of a public health perspective is to understand these three types of factors as interacting with each other. Whereas the history of the alcoholism field has been one of rivalry among such perspectives for supremacy (Is alcoholism caused by alcohol *or* by susceptibility *or* by the environment?), public health professionals recognize the contribution of each factor to a complex disease process. Host and environmental variables become *risk factors* which, when combined with the agent, influence the level of disease. Asserting the importance of one factor (e.g., behavior or environment) does not logically require that one eschew the importance of another (e.g., genetic susceptibility). Current major diseases (e.g., hypertension, diabetes, heart disease, cancer) are best understood as interactions of host, agent, and environmental influences. In this sense, alcohol problems resemble complex disease processes.

The model of alcohol problems that one embraces is a crucial determinant of the types of intervention that one will entertain. Attempts to control the availability of alcohol within a population do not readily follow from an American disease model which attributes alcohol problems to a unique constitutional susceptibility. Interventions which seem central from the perspective of one model may appear fruitless or at least extremely limited from another perspective.

Implications for Programming

Thus far we have offered a blending of theory and outcome research. The conceptual model of motivation discussed earlier emphasized the importance of two factors as catalysts of change: perception of risk and self-efficacy for change. Several strategies for impacting these two factors have been suggested. How might these strategies be turned into practical programs on a college campus?

With the help of a grant from the Fund for the Improvement of Higher Education, U.S. Department of Education (No. G008730491), we designed a program to do just that. Our overall goals were (1) to increase awareness of risks inherent in hazardous drinking and drug use practices, and (2) to provide a variety of response alternatives through which change might be pursued. Our target group was the entire campus population of the University of New Mexico (UNM), comprising more than 24,000 students and 6,000 faculty and staff. The population of the university is a multicultural mix of anglo, hispanic, native American, black, and asian groups from urban and rural environments. UNM students, with an average age of twenty-seven, are largely commuters, with fewer than 10 percent living on campus. The State of New Mexico in general ranks very high in morbidity and mortality related to alcohol and other drug abuse.

The Campus Alcohol and Drug Abuse Prevention Program (CADAPP) at UNM is based on the motivational model described above, offering a comprehensive, campus-wide approach to prevention programming. Our challenge in implementing CADAPP was to effect change at the individual, group, and institutional levels, and to work toward the integration of prevention components into the ongoing university curricular and support programs. To meet this challenge, CADAPP initially included eleven component strategies, encompassing both large scale (macro) and individual (micro) interventions to address alcohol and other drug abuse.

Though founded on a cognitive-motivational model, the objectives of CADAPP are clearly definable in behavioral terms. It was designed to: (1) promote non-use as a valid and desirable lifestyle choice, encouraging non-users to continue in this pattern; (2) persuade at-risk users to alter their use of alcohol and other drugs; and (3) discourage the use, even in moderation, of alcohol or other drugs in high-risk situations (e.g., in association with driving).

Each of the eleven initial components translated motivational theory into programmatic content by attempting to impact either awareness of risk or development of alternatives. These components of CADAPP were divided into two tiers: primary prevention strategies, and secondary prevention strategies.

Primary Prevention Strategies

Primary prevention strategies have a more macro focus, attempting to impact the entire campus population by increasing risk awareness and promoting alternatives to alcohol and drug use. CADAPP initially included seven primary prevention strategies.

1. *Print Media.* This component disseminated motivational messages through a variety of print media likely to be read by large segments of the campus population. These included a bi-weekly column in the campus newspaper, an enclosure in the semester schedule of classes, and posters in high traffic areas. Attractive materials were published for general distribution, including a resource card listing names and telephone numbers of campus services, and a "College Survival Handbook" offering coping strategies for situations that are common antecedents of alcohol or drug use.

2. *Electronic Media.* A variety of videotapes were developed for use in classrooms, in campus service centers (such as the Wellness Center), and during student orientation and campus tours.

3. *Computer Resources.* Utilizing both the mainframe and microcomputer resources of the university is a high tech strategy for reaching the students, faculty, and staff who use these systems. Interactive programs were installed to provide information, games, and personal feedback. These programs offered services such as the generation of a personalized blood alcohol concentration table and a confidential health risk appraisal.

4. *Classroom.* Prevention programs that can be integrated into classroom instruction are more likely to endure the vicissitudes of prevention funding. We developed and implemented a credit course entitled "Coping with College." Using videotapes, live instruction, role plays, and the College Survival Handbook, this course taught practical skills for negotiating the transitions and challenges of university life. Topics covered included time management, stress reduction, communication and assertion skills, mood management, study skills, and personal health care. Information on alcohol and other drug problems was integrated, but the primary strategy was to teach alternatives to drugs in coping with situations and challenges commonly associated with substance use and abuse.

A second classroom strategy was the development of a teaching resource center on alcohol and other drugs. This center was planned to serve faculty and teaching assistants seeking current information to integrate into new and existing courses. In addition to a research library on addictive behaviors, we are developing a set of videotapes and brief updated information sheets on high interest topics.

5. *Alcohol and Substance Abuse Prevention Program (ASAP).* In constructing CADAPP, we worked in cooperation with an innovative prevention program already on campus. The ASAP program is an experientially based approach to understanding alcohol and other drug use/abuse at both the societal and the individual level. Through interviews conducted at a local hospital, emergency room, and county jail, students use

a problem-posing method to explore alcohol and other drug problems. Ultimately, student participants in ASAP are asked to return to their community (in our case, the university) and take on the role of peer educator, sharing their experiences and applying the problem-posing method. This approach has been previously tested and found successful with secondary school students (Bernstein & Woodall, 1987), and is now being extended to the university student population through CADAPP.

6. *Public Lectures.* A traditional component of primary prevention programs is educational lectures. We sponsored an ongoing series of public lectures on alcohol and other drug problems. Major speakers within the CADAPP model focused on one or both of the motivational themes: awareness of risk, and development of alternatives.

7. *Policy Development.* Any campus-wide prevention program should be consonant and integrated with the university's official policies on alcohol/drug use and problems. UNM completed a comprehensive review of its policy on alcohol and other drugs with CADAPP staff providing consultation in this process. A university policy should clearly reflect the institution's values and rules with regard to alcohol and other drugs, and define the consequences of violations of the policy. The UNM policy focuses not only on individual behavior, but also on larger issues such as the liability of those who serve alcohol, responsible server practices, and the advertising and promotion of alcoholic beverages on campus.

Secondary Prevention

The secondary prevention tier of CADAPP initially included four strategies. These were designed to target high-risk individuals within the campus population.

8. *Drinker's Check-up.* As part of CADAPP, the Drinker's Check-up (described earlier in this chapter) was made available free of charge to all UNM faculty, students, staff, and their family members (Miller, Sovereign, & Krege, 1988). It was advertised as a confidential check-up for people who would like to know whether they are being harmed by their use of alcohol or other

drugs. It was explicitly stated that the check-up is not part of any treatment program, and that the individual would not be labelled. The service was offered on campus through the Department of Psychology Clinic.

9. *Peer Counseling.* Strengthening and augmenting existing student and staff counseling services was the focus of this component. The goal was to train "natural helpers" within the university system to provide peer counseling services (Christensen, Miller, & Muñoz, 1978). Specialized training was offered in the recognition of at-risk patterns of use and in motivational strategies for intervention.

10. *Referral.* To assist in making appropriate referrals to community resources, we conducted a survey of all available programs offering prevention and treatment services for alcohol and other drug problems within our metropolitan area. These were then described in a resource directory which was provided to multiple campus sites from which referrals might be made.

11. *Concerned Others.* Still another potential target population consists of the friends and relatives of people with alcohol and other drug problems. These concerned others frequently wish to intervene in a helpful manner, but lack the needed knowledge or skills to do so effectively. A program was implemented to support and train concerned others in effective motivational intervention strategies (Miller & Rollnick, 1991; Sisson & Azrin, 1986).

Increasing Perception of Risk

A common goal of these intervention strategies was to increase individual and institutional awareness of risk. Alcohol was presented as a drug that poses risk for all who use it beyond moderation, not only for a few with unique susceptibility. Emphasis was placed on information linking alcohol and other drug use to outcomes of immediate concern: academic and career success, injury and disability, and personal health.

The concept of risk was specifically not limited to the long-term effects of chronic use. Many tragic outcomes result not from prolonged excess, but from unwise use in a single situation. There are no known safe blood levels of alcohol or other drugs when driving, using power tools, swimming and boating, or using firearms (e.g., when hunting). An early theme of CADAPP was "Zero Behind the Wheel." The central idea of this campaign is that the only safe blood alcohol level while driving is zero. Any drinking before driving, therefore, should be planned so that enough time has elapsed to eliminate all alcohol prior to driving. Simple informational cards were provided to assist people in determining the length of time required to metabolize various amounts of alcohol. Other risks of acute intoxication include overdose, unwise risk-taking, and loss of behavioral control.

The legal risks involved in illicit drug use represented a third emphasis. In an era of drug testing and increased sensitivity to substance use issues, a single legal incident involving drugs can have long-term repercussions on one's career. A large percentage of criminal offenses against persons are committed under the influence of alcohol and other drugs.

In discussing risk, it is also sensible to include information about risk factors. There are impressive individual differences in susceptibility to alcohol and other drug problems based on family history, age, gender, racial/cultural heritage, occupation, and subculture. Prevention programming can address these specific risk factors, as well as general risks attached to acute and chronic use.

A comprehensive prevention program, then, addresses this larger pattern of risks associated with alcohol and other drugs. The strategies need not extend to the excesses of unrealistic "scare tactics." The objective, accurate information about risks is sobering enough. First hand information (e.g., obtained from a survey on one's own campus) may be particularly persuasive. We were able, based on our own survey, to show a relationship between alcohol abuse and poor grades, and to associate certain reasons for drinking (e.g., to get high, or for emotional coping) with a high risk for problems.

Alternatives to Use

A "just say no" strategy is likely to fall short in failing to recognize that alcohol and other drug use is a motivated behavior, often serving coping functions (Miller & Pechacek, 1987). The most commonly mentioned motivation for use was the same among our students, faculty, and staff: to relax. The primary motivation for use, as stated by the individual, proved in our survey to be a strong marker of risk. Defining an alcohol problem based on responses to World Health Organization screening items (Saunders & Aasland, 1987), the lowest risk group was those drinking because they "like the taste" (3.5% with significant alcohol problems). Those drinking "to relax" showed twice the risk (7.1%), as did those drinking "to feel more comfortable and outgoing in social situations" (8.7%). The highest risk, however, was attached to drinking "to get high" (33.3%) and for emotional coping purposes (35.6% overall) such as "to feel happier" (43.8%), "to forget about my problems" (50%), or "to deal with loneliness" (57.1%). One-third to one-half of those designating such primary reasons for their drinking fell within the problem range on the WHO scale.

Raising awareness of risk is not enough. The protection motivation model described above would predict that risk enhancement alone would lead not to behavior change, but to defensiveness. A comprehensive prevention program includes strategies to promote alternatives to the use of alcohol and other drugs for coping purposes.

These alternatives should be considerably wider than the traditional "get help" option. Our research with the Drinker's Check-up indicates that a substantial percentage of people can and do change their drinking behavior on their own without formal help when given a brief motivational intervention. A menu of readily accessible alternative strategies is an important component when addressing drug abuse.

A first step is to identify, within one's own population, the most common motivations for use and abuse. A well-designed campus survey can serve this function. Assuming that these turn out to be problems with which individuals must somehow cope, prevention programming can then be addressed to teaching drug-free coping skills. This is an explicit goal in many of the prevention strategies discussed earlier (e.g., print, electronic, classroom).

Results of the Program

We evaluated CADAPP by conducting random sample surveys of university students, faculty, and staff at two points: at the beginning of the fall term just before implementation of CADAPP, and again a year and a half later at the end of spring term, with CADAPP fully implemented. Another large public university in New Mexico served as a control campus, administering surveys at the same points with no new prevention programming implemented in between. Relative to the control campus, random survey data from students on the CADAPP campus showed significantly decreased quantity and frequency of drinking, lower rates of driving after drinking, and decreased use of illicit drugs in general and marijuana in particular. The CADAPP campus also showed significantly increased perception of risks of alcohol/drug use relative to the control campus, and decreased rates of riding with an intoxicated driver. It appears, therefore, that CADAPP had the intended effect of increasing risk perceptions and decreasing alcohol/drug use and related risk behaviors (Miller, Miller, & Toscova, 1990).

Summary

We have presented a conceptual model, based on motivational principles and research, that can be used to guide programs for the prevention of alcohol and other drug problems in young adults. The model emphasizes combined strategies to increase risk perception and teach alternative coping skills. Successful drug abuse prevention efforts using this combination of strategies have already been reported (e.g., Botvin et al., 1984). Within a heterogeneous population such as a university, no single strategy is likely to have a major impact on problem incidence. Combinations of strategies, guided by a unifying conceptual model, may prove optimal in impacting motivational variables that precede the use and abuse of alcohol and other drugs.

References

Alcoholics Anonymous (1976). *Alcoholics Anonymous: The story of how many thousands of men and women have recovered from alcoholism.* (Rev. ed.) New York.

Bandura, A. (1982). Self-efficacy mechanism in human agency. *American Psychologist, 37,* 12–-147.

Bernstein, E., & Woodall, G. (1987). Changing perceptions of riskiness in drinking, drugs, and driving: An emergency department-based alcohol and substance abuse prevention program. *Annals of Emergency Medicine, 16,* 1350–1354.

Botvin, G. J., Baker, E., Renick, N. L., Fillazola, A. D., & Botvin, E. M. (1984). A cognitive-behavioral approach to substance abuse prevention. *Addictive Behaviors, 9,* 137–147.

Burnum, J. F. (1984). Outlook for treating patients with self-destructive habits. *Annals of Internal Medicine, 81,* 387–393.

Cahalan, D. (1987). *Understanding America's drinking problem: How to combat the hazards of alcohol.* San Francisco: Jossey-Bass.

Chafetz, M. E. (1961). A procedure for establishing therapeutic contact with the alcoholic. *Quarterly Journal of Studies on Alcohol, 22,* 325–328.

Chick, J., Ritson, B., Connaughton, J., Stewart, A., & Chick, J. (1988). Advice versus extended treatment for alcoholism: A controlled study. *British Journal of Addiction, 83,* 159–170.

Christensen, A., Miller, W. R., & Muñoz, R. F. (1978). Para-professionals, partners, peers, paraphernalia, and print: Expanding mental health service delivery. *Professional Psychology, 9,* 249–270.

Deci, E. L. (1975). *Intrinsic motivation.* New York: Plenum.

Edwards, G., Orford, J., Egert, S., Guthrie, S., Hawker, A., Hensman, C., Mitcheson, M., Oppenheimer, E., & Taylor, C. (1977). Alcoholism: A controlled trial of "treatment" and "advice." *Journal of Studies on Alcohol, 38,* 1004–1031.

Elvy, G. A., Wells, J. E., & Baird, K. A. (1988). Attempted referral as intervention for problem drinkers. *British Journal of Addiction, 83.* 83–89.

Ends, E. J., & Page, C. W. (1957). A study of three types of group psychotherapy with hospitalized male inebriates. *Quarterly Journal of Studies on Alcohol, 18,* 263–277.

Fingarette, H. (1988). *Heavy drinking: The myth of alcoholism as a disease.* Berkeley: University of California Press.

Heather, N. (1986). Change without therapists: The use of self-help manuals by problem drinkers. In W. R. Miller & N. Heather (Eds.), *Treating addictive behaviors: Processes of change.* New York: Plenum Press.

Heather, N., & Robertson, I. (1983). *Controlled drinking* (Rev. ed.). London: Methuen.

Heather, N., Whitton, B., & Robertson, I. (1986). Evaluation of a self-help manual for media-recruited problem drinkers: Six month follow-up results. *British Journal of Clinical Psychology, 25.* 19–34.

Holder, H., Longabaugh, R., Miller, W. R., & Rubonis, A. V. (1991). The cost effectiveness of treatment for alcoholism: A first approximation. *Journal of Studies on Alcohol, 52,* 517–540.

Institute of Medicine, National Academy of Sciences (1990). *Broadening the base of treatment for alcohol problems.* Washington, DC: National Academy Press.

Jellinek, E. M. (1960). *The disease concept of alcoholism.* New Haven: Hillhouse Press.

Kopel, S., & Arkowitz, H. (1975). The role of attribution and self-perception in behavior change: Implications for behavior therapy. *Genetic Psychology Monographs, 92,* 175–212.

Kristenson, H. (1983). *Studies on alcohol related disabilities in a medical intervention* (2nd ed.). Malmö, Sweden: University of Lund.

Leake, G. J., & King, A. S. (1977). Effect of counselor expectations on alcoholic recovery. *Alcohol Health and Research World, 11* (3), 16–22.

Miller, W. R. (1983). Motivational interviewing with problem drinkers. *Behavioural Psychotherapy, 11,* 147–172.

Miller, W. R. (1985). Motivation for treatment: A review with special emphasis on alcoholism. *Psychological Bulletin, 98,* 84–107.

Miller, W. R. (1987). Motivation and treatment goals. *Drugs and Society, 1,* 133–151.

Miller, W. R., & Baca, L. M. (1983). Two-year follow-up of bibliotherapy and therapist-directed controlled drinking training for problem drinkers. *Behavior Therapy, 14,* 441–448.

Miller, W. R., Benefield, R. G., & Tonigan, J. S. (1993). Enhancing motivation for change in problem drinking: A controlled comparison of two therapist styles. *Journal of Consulting and Clinical Psychology, 61,* 455–461.

Miller, W. R., & Hester, R. K. (1986). Matching problem drinkers with optimal treatment methods. In W. R. Miller & N. Heather (Eds.), *Treating addictive behaviors: Processes of change.* New York: Plenum Press.

Miller, W. R., & Hester, R. K. (1989). Treating alcohol problems: Toward an informed eclecticism. In R. K. Hester & W. R. Miller (Eds.), *Handbook of alcoholism treatment aproaches: Effective alternatives.* Elmsford, N.Y.: Pergamon Press.

Miller, B., Miller, W. R., & Toscova, R. (1990). Final report: The University of New Mexico Campus Alcohol and Drug Abuse Prevention program (CADAPP). Report to the U.S. Department of Education (Grant #G008730491).

Miller, W. R., & Muñoz, R. F. (1982). *How to control your drinking.* (Rev. ed.) Albuquerque: University of New Mexico Press.

Miller, W. R., & Pechacek, T. F. (1987). New roads: Assessing and treating psychological dependence. *Journal of Substance Abuse Treatment, 4,* 73–77.

Miller, W. R., & Rollnick, S. (1991). *Motivational interviewing: Preparing people to change addictive behavior.* New York: Guilford Press.

Miller, W. R., Sovereign, R. G., & Krege, B. (1988). Motivational interviewing with problem drinkers: II. The Drinker's Check-up as a preventive intervention. *Behavioural Psychotherapy, 16,* 251–268.

Miller, W. R., Taylor, C. A., & West, J. C. (1980). Focused versus broad-spectrum behavior therapy for problem drinkers. *Journal of Consulting and Clinical Psychology, 48,* 590–601.

Milmoe, S., Rosenthal, R., Blane, H. T., Chafetz, M. E., & Wolf, I.

(1967). The doctor's voice: Postdictor of successful referral of alcoholic patients. *Journal of Abnormal Psychology, 72*, 78–84.

Moore, M. H., & Gerstein, D. R. (1981). *Alcohol and public policy: Beyond the shadow of Prohibition.* Washington, D.C.: National Academy Press.

Prochaska, J. O., & DiClemente, C. C. (1982). Transtheoretical therapy: Toward a more integrative model of change. *Psychotherapy: Theory, Research, and Practice, 19*, 276–288.

Prochaska, J. O., & DiClemente, C. C. (1986). Toward a comprehensive model of change. In W. R. Miller & N. Heather (Eds.), *Treating addictive behaviors: Processes of change.* New York: Plenum Press.

Ritson, B. (1986). The merits of simple intervention. In W. R. Miller & N. Heather (Eds.), *Treating addictive behaviors: Processes of change.* New York: Plenum Press.

Robertson, I., Heather, N., Dzialdowski, A., Crawford, J., & Winton, M. (1986). A comparison of minimal versus intensive treatment interventions for problem drinkers. *British Journal of Clinical Psychology, 25*, 185–194.

Rogers, R. W. (1975). A protection motivation theory of fear appeals and attitude change. *Journal of Psychology, 91*, 93–114.

Rogers, R. W., Deckner, C. W., & Mewborn, C. R. (1978) An expectancy-value theory approach to the long-term modification of smoking behavior. *Journal of Clinical Psychology, 34*, 562–566.

Rogers, R. W., & Mewborn, C. R. (1976). Fear appeals and attitude change: Effects of a threat's noxiousness, probability of occurrence, and the efficacy of coping responses. *Journal of Personality and Social Psychology, 34*, 54–61.

Russell, M. A. H., Wilson, C., Taylor, C., & Baker, C. D. (1979). Effects of general practitioners' advice against smoking. *British Medical Journal, 2*, 231–235.

Saunders, J. B., & Aasland, O. G. (1987). *WHO collaborative project on identification and treatment of persons with harmful alcohol consumption: Report on Phase I: Development of a screening instrument*. Geneva: World Health Organization, Division of Mental Health.

Sisson, R. W., & Azrin, N. H. (1986). Family-member involvement to initiate and promote treatment of problem drinkers. *Journal of Behavior Therapy and Experimental Psychiatry, 17,* 15–21.

Truax, C. B., & Carkhuff, R. R. (1967). *Toward effective counseling and psychotherapy.* Chicago: Aldine.

Vaillant, G. M. (1983). *The natural history of alcoholism: Causes patterns, and paths to recovery.* Cambridge, Mass.: Harvard University Press.

Valle, S. K. (1981). Interpersonal functioning of alcoholism counselors and treatment outcome. *Journal of Studies on Alcohol, 42,* 783–790.

Secondary Prevention of Alcohol Abuse with College Student Populations: A Skills-Training Approach

John S. Baer, Daniel R. Kivlahan, Kim Fromme, and G. Alan Marlatt

Problems associated with college student drinking have been documented in a number of reviews (Berkowitz & Perkins, 1986; Saltz & Elandt, 1986; Walfish et al., 1981). Surveys suggest that most (70% to 95%) students drink; an estimated 15 to 25 percent are classified as heavy or problem drinkers. Alcohol is a central agent in a variety of behavioral problems exhibited by college students, including driving while intoxicated, poor academic performance, vandalism, and aggression. Accidents involving alcohol are the major cause of death for persons aged sixteen to twenty-four (NIAAA, 1984). The problem of student alcohol abuse has become so extensive that almost every college in the USA now has, or is considering, an alcohol program. Such concerns for drinking problems are shared by administrators and student groups (Gonzalez, 1981; Sherwood, 1987).

Despite this concern about college student drinking practices, a number of barriers inhibit developing effective prevention and early intervention programs. Resistance is encountered at administrative, social, and personal levels. Administratively, there is legal concern for admitting (and condoning) that persons drink under the legal age of twenty-one. For example, the National Council on Alcoholism and NIAAA have opposed responsible drinking as a treatment or prevention goal for those under twenty-one. Yet, few would argue that abstinence until age twenty-one is a viable social solution. Typical programs end up detailing risks associated with alcohol consumption, implicitly suggesting one should not drink, while recognizing that most students do drink.

Socially, negative stigma is associated with 'alcohol problems' and 'alcoholism,' thus reducing participation when programs are offered. Many groups incorrectly believe that only addicted drinkers have social problems like driving while intoxicated or alcohol-related accidents. In fact, most heavy student drinkers do not qualify as 'alcoholics' in the traditional sense (Institute of Medicine, 1990).

On a personal level, most college students do not see their drinking as a problem. To admit to a problem with alcohol necessitates acknowledgment of lack of control (failure), and perhaps the acceptance of life-long abstinence. College drinking usually occurs in social "party" situations over short periods of time. Many students believe their college years are a time to be irresponsible and reckless, and that safer drinking will later develop naturally. Within this social climate, most programs have been information-oriented; few have been carefully evaluated.

The continuing research described in this chapter represents an effort to develop techniques for reducing the risks associated with college student drinking patterns in light of the barriers noted above. In short, we have developed a research-based risk-reduction program that focuses on self-control or self-management skills. Our program is designed to encourage participation by being non-judgmental, and to promote real changes in drinking behavior by offering more than just information about risks associated with drinking. We acknowledge widespread drinking (and unsafe drinking) by underage individuals. Program content is based on cognitive-behavioral self-management strategies and research on the psychological aspects of alcohol effects. Low-risk drinking strategies are openly described. We have also attempted to carefully evaluate our program in comparison to control groups and for cost effectiveness.

The rationale and specific content of the Alcohol Skills Training Program is described below, along with preliminary results of our research efforts. We conclude this chapter with a discussion of critical clinical issues related to working with this population and offer some suggestions for future research.

Rationale for a Skills Training Program

The rationale for an alcohol skills training program with college students derives from several trends in psychological and alcohol research: the failure of purely informational campaigns to effect change in drinking behavior, the growing understanding of the social and cognitive determinants of drinking, and the success of cognitive-behavioral skills training programs with other populations of drinkers. Each will be briefly detailed below.

The most important measure of any intervention program must be that of its success in changing behavior. Unfortunately, the track record of most existing primary prevention programs for college student drinking is poor. Few programs include adequate experimental design or follow-up evaluation (Goodstadt, 1986). Even programs with outcome evaluations do not usually produce desired changes in drinking behavior. For example, two well-designed programs that involved careful organization and multi-stage, campus-wide information dissemination were successful in changing attitudes and knowledge about alcohol, yet did not result in significant reductions in drinking (Kraft, 1984; Mills & McCarty, 1983). These results are consistent with those from school-based primary prevention programs, which seldom result in changes in drug and alcohol use (Mauss et al., 1988; Moskowitz, 1989).

Information programs are based on the unsubstantiated notion that change in attitudes alone is sufficient to change behavior. More encouraging results have been reported with alcohol programs that involve college students in specific cognitive training exercises and/or field experiences (Goodstadt & Caleekal-John, 1984; Rozelle, 1980).

Research in our laboratory has shown that the power of

social norms, peer groups, and perceived alcohol effects are strong. Consumption of alcohol is determined by the consumption rate and sex of peer models (Collins & Marlatt, 1981), specific emotional states (Marlatt, 1987), relaxation and aerobic exercise (Murphy, Pagano, & Marlatt, 1986), and beliefs and misperceptions about alcohol effects (Lang & Marlatt, 1983). Alcohol consumption is intimately involved in the normal social and psychological factors found in collegiate settings.

Our research suggests that college student drinkers may need both specific skills and knowledge about applications of new social behaviors to effectively change high-risk drinking behavior. For example, although students may be aware that consuming large amounts of alcohol is dangerous, they may be unable or unwilling to reduce their risk unless they feel that they can effectively cope with social pressure, the desire to relax, or the desire to fit in. Indeed, making effective choices about drinking may require the ability and willingness to cope with drinking situations in new ways. Possessing factual information alone is insufficient.

Social learning interventions are designed to provide people with an understanding of their behavior patterns and the requisite control necessary to implement new behaviors. In the field of alcohol treatment, several research programs have developed techniques for assisting problem drinkers in abstaining or moderating their use of alcohol (Hay & Nathan, 1982; Marlatt & Nathan, 1978; Miller, 1976). Treatment strategies usually include self-monitoring of drinking, understanding blood alcohol levels (BAL) and effects, systematically evaluating situations in which drinking occurs, and planning specific strategies for coping with high-risk situations. Systematic research with these procedures has demonstrated minimization of relapse in chronic alcoholics (Chaney, O'Leary, & Marlatt, 1978), and significant reductions in drinking among younger problem drinkers (Alden, 1988; Sanchez-Craig et al., 1984).

The Alcohol Skills Training Program is designed to provide college students with specific recommendations on how to reduce risks associated with heavy drinking. In addition to providing knowledge about risks associated with alcohol, we seek to give students specific strategies for changing drinking behavior. Strategies focus on improving understanding of personal drinking habits, awareness of blood alcohol levels and typical alcohol effects, and refuting common myths about the power of alcohol in social situations. Students are taught to evaluate social and psychological motivations for drinking (e.g., social ease, celebration, relaxation), and to plan alternative solutions. Naturally, people can choose to refrain from drinking altogether.

Our work with college student drinkers can also be placed in a developmental context of how alcohol problems change across the life span. Epidemiological data suggest that alcohol problems associated with the college years are usually quite distinct from addictive drinking patterns typically found in middle age (Fillmore, Bacon, & Hyman, 1979; Fillmore & Midanik, 1984). Over 65 percent of those showing signs of alcohol problems in their late teens and early twenties moderate their drinking patterns by their late twenties as life situations and demands change. During their early period of heavy drinking, individuals are at high-risk for accidents (noted earlier), as well as poor occupational and social adjustment. Our intervention efforts can be considered as an attempt to 'speed up' the process of maturation. Because our program is not conceptualized as a treatment for alcohol addiction, students showing signs of physical dependency are referred for abstinence-orientated treatment (see below). However, secondary prevention can be useful for individuals characterized as early stage problem or abusive drinkers. This population has been shown to be most responsive to moderate drinking programs (Miller & Hester, 1986; Sanchez-Craig et al., 1984).

Our initial study assessed the efficacy of a skills training program presented as an eight-week class for college students. This class was compared to both an Alcohol Information School, offered by the State of Washington for first time drunk-driving offenders, and an assessment-only control group. Later studies have examined the cost-effectiveness of skills training presented in different program formats. Our research efforts have given us increasing insight into the complexities of changing drinking behavior among student populations. The remainder of this chapter describes our program, presents some encouraging results, and offers suggestions for future research.

Study I: Skills Training vs. Alcohol Information School and Assessment Only Control

This first test of a skills training approach involved the development of the Alcohol Skills Training Program (ASTP), recruiting and screening all participants, and assessing program effectiveness by comparing it to a traditional alcohol information program and to an assessment-only control group. Of critical concern was the acceptability of the program to students and the potential impact on actual drinking behavior (in addition to acquisition of new knowledge). As the design and results of this first study have been reported elsewhere (Kivlahan et al., 1990), they will be described only briefly here.

Design

Prospective subjects were recruited by fliers, campus newspaper advertisements, class announcements, and at sign-up booths in the University of Washington student union. Newspaper advertisements noting payment for research activity were the most productive recruitment strategy. An eight-week educational program was offered for social drinkers wanting to learn more about or change their drinking patterns. Subjects were randomly assigned to one of three experimental conditions: (a) Alcohol Skills Training Program (ASTP), (b) Alcohol Information School, or (c) Assessment-Only Control. In addition, subjects agreed to complete follow-up assessment periodically for one year. Each was paid $50 for participating. Because the ASTP was designed for high-risk drinkers, we screened out students showing signs of alcohol dependency, as well as those showing minimal evidence of drinking risks. To qualify subjects needed (a) to score in the medium volume/high maximum or high volume/high maximum categories of Cahalan's (Cahalan & Room, 1974) volume variability index; (b) to have a least one negative consequence of drinking, as assessed with the Michigan Alcohol Screening Test (MAST; Selzer, 1971); and (c) score 13 or below on the Alcohol Dependence Scale (ADS; Horn et al., 1984), indicating no more than mild physical dependence symptoms.

Program Content

Alcohol Skills Training Program (ASTP). A psychoeducational model was adopted, using didactic presentations and small group discussions as a means of communicating cognitive-behavioral principles. Program classes were administered once a week for eight weeks and had approximately eight members. Groups were led by male and female co-leaders, three of whom were doctoral-level clinical psychologists, and the other an advanced clinical psychology graduate student. During each session, participants described and discussed their experiences in self-monitoring drinking and other weekly homework assignments. Besides presenting information about alcohol and its effects, the ASTP attempted to foster decision-making and self-management skills.

Each weekly session focused on a specific topic: (1) models of addiction and effects of drinking; (2) estimating Blood Alcohol Levels (BAL) and gaining skills to maintain set drinking limits; (3) relaxation training and lifestyle balance; (4) nutritional information and aerobic exercise; (5) antecedents of drinking and coping with high-risk situations; (6) assertiveness training and drink refusal; (7) placebo drinking session in a simulated tavern; and (8) relapse prevention strategies for maintaining behavior changes. Session 7 was the unique aspect of the ASTP. In a simulated tavern, nonalcoholic (placebo) drinks were given to subjects who believed they were participating in a test for alcohol effects (subjects believed they were drinking alcohol). After approximately thirty minutes of drinking and discussion, subjects were asked to describe the effects of drinking and to state how confident they felt that their drinks contained alcohol.

The purpose of this session was to discuss the psychological effects of alcohol and the power of personal expectancies and beliefs.

Alcohol Information School (AIS). The AIS was based on the program required by the State of Washington for those convicted of under-age possession of alcohol or driving under the influence of alcohol. Groups met once a week for eight weeks, and consisted of didactic presentations about alcohol effects, problems associated with alcohol, and alcoholism as a disease. The program was taught by a licensed AIS instructor, and was assisted by an advanced graduate student in physiological psychology. Lecture topics included (1) dispelling myths about alcohol; (2) physical and behavioral effects of alcohol; (3) effects of drug interaction with alcohol; (4) the alcohol industry; (5) alcoholism; (6) alcoholism and the family; (7) alcoholism and the law; and (8) responsible decision making about alcohol consumption. Subjects were not presented with or trained in any cognitive-behavioral or lifestyle/stress-management skills.

Assessment-Only Control. The Assessment-Only control group was included to test for nonspecific effects of participation in the research program. We were particularly interested in assessing the effect of having subjects complete assessment forms and self-monitor their drinking over an extended period of time. The Assessment-Only control group provided data for comparing the more detailed interventions described above. Students in this group completed all screening and research scales, and monitored their drinking for the same eight-week period during which the other programs were offered. Although no intervention was offered to subjects in this condition, subjects were offered the ASTP after the one follow-up.

Subjects in Study I

The sample of 43 individuals who completed the eight-week program was 58 percent male and averaged twenty-three years of age. Drinking assessments at baseline (pre-treatment) clearly revealed a pattern of high-risk drinking behavior. The lifetime maximum drinks per occasion averaged 16.6; an average of 7.5 driving occasions after consumption of four or more drinks over the past year was reported. Based on Cahalan's Drinking Habits Questionnaire, subjects consumed 15.1 drinks per week. Twenty-eight percent of the sample reported parental history of alcohol problems.

Results of Study I

The impact of the ASTP was assessed by students' evaluations of the program, self-monitored drinking rates, and estimates of weekly drinking rates (Drinking Habits Questionnaire). Baseline measures were re-assessed at the end of the program and at three occasions over a one-year follow-up period. Self-monitored drinking was scored with a computer program developed by Mathews and Miller (1979). This program computed (among other variables) the number of standard drinks per week (standard ethanol consumption units; SECs) and the peak blood alcohol level reached each week (PBAL).

From pre- to post-program, results from the drinking measures from the 43 subjects indicate significant reductions in number of SECs per week and PBAL for all participants. On average, students drank 16.4 SECs before the program, and 12.5 after. Weekly PBAL from pre- to post-treatment declined similarly, from 0.13 to 0.10 percent.

Figure 1 compares treatment groups across all assessment for the self-monitoring measures. The largest changes from pre- to post-treatment were found in the ASTP; 38.5 percent reduction in drinks consumed, and 47.3 percent reduction in PBAL. The Information School reduced by 21.6 percent in SECs and 21.5 percent in PBAL in comparison. Although suggestive these differences were not statistically significant.

As Figure 1 shows, follow-up assessments at twelve months revealed general maintenance of the gains made during the program, again with subjects in the ASTP drinking least; of the 43 subjects, 36 provided complete follow-up data. At the one-year follow-up, ASTP subjects reported 6.6 SECs per week, and

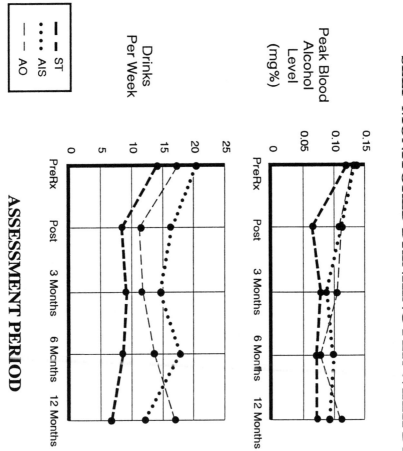

SELF-MONITORED DRINKING PER WEEK BY GROUP

ASSESSMENT PERIOD

0.07 percent PBAL, compared to 12.7 SECs, and 0.09 percent PBAL, and 16.8 SECs, and 0.11 percent PBAL for the AIS and Control groups, respectively.

Measures of self-perceived drinking patterns, in which subjects generalized over a ninety-day period, show subjects in the ASTP to have reduced their drinking significantly more than the other two groups when assessed at the one-year follow-up. At the one-year follow-up, ASTP subjects estimated their change in drinking at 7.9 drinks per week less, whereas participants in the other groups estimated their drinking to have either increased (4.0 drinks greater in the control group), or to have remained the same (AIS group).

These initial results, although not consistent differences between treatment conditions, were still encouraging. Students actively involved in a research program significantly reduced their drinking. At each follow-up, subjects in the ASTP showed the greatest changes. The sample size of the study was limited, thus reducing power of the study to find statistical differences among treatment groups. Impact varied. Some individuals reported no changes, and even those who changed on average continued to report isolated incidents of heavy drinking. Perhaps most important, we were able to develop a skills training program that was well received by students once they decided to participate. Subject recruitment was difficult; as expected, students failed to respond to an invitation to participate in an 'alcohol program.' Once engaged, however, feedback indicated that the ASTP was perceived as just as helpful as typical alcohol education programs.

Study II: A Comparison of Methods of Intervention: Cost-Effectiveness

The second trial of our alcohol skills-training approach was designed to evaluate different methods of administrating the ASTP with a focus on cost-effectiveness. Encouraged by the results of Study I, we sought first to replicate the magnitude of drinking reductions. We also sought to dismantle the group treatment to evaluate different program formats, seeking to find the most efficient means of attaining behavioral changes.

One advantage to the group setting of the ASTP was that group members were able to share common experiences and thus form a basis for support and encouragement. Using a group setting, therefore, may produce the best treatment results. Conversely, group programs can be expensive if professional time and overhead costs are considered. The same material, in a written, self-help format, could be a more efficient or cost-effective means of administering a drinking-skills program. Indeed, previous research has suggested that self-help materials can be as effective as group or individual treatment for alcohol-related problems (Heather, Whitton, & Robertson, 1986; Miller & Taylor, 1980).

In a study by Orford and Edwards (1977), it was found that a brief, one-hour advice session by a physician was as effective as more intensive treatment at a one-year follow-up. Because an important component of the ASTP is the monitoring and studying of personal drinking habits, perhaps personalized professional advice (based on feedback from a comprehensive assessment) is sufficient to motivate college students to change their drinking practices.

After evaluating these issues, we developed a random-ized study comparing three methods of administering the basic content of the ASTP: (1) group treatment, (2) a self-paced correspondence course, and (3) one session of individualized advice and feedback (with no additional training). Complete results from Study II are described elsewhere (Baer et al., 1991), and, similar to Study I, only the essential findings are reported here. In order to assess more long-term effects of the intervention, a two-year follow-up period was included.

Design

Student volunteers were recruited by fliers and newspaper advertisements to participate in a six-week, skills training program offered to those who wanted to learn more about or to change their drinking patterns. As in Study I, notices containing information about monetary compensation for research participation produced the best results. Subjects were asked to agree to complete assessments at pre-program, post-program, and intermittently over a two-year follow-up period, and to monitor their drinking during the six-week program. Students were paid $75 (over six installments) for participating. Subjects also agreed to be randomly assigned to one of three program formats: (1) a six-week class program, meeting once a week in small groups; (2) a self-paced, six-unit correspondence course; or (3) a single, one-hour feedback session after baseline assessment was completed. Criteria for acceptance into the research program were more inclusive than in the initial study. Subjects needed to report a MAST score of at least 1, at least two days drinking in an average week, with blood alcohol levels approaching 0.10 percent. Subjects who reported MAST scores above 10 and Physical Dependency (Marlatt & Miller, 1984) scores above 5 were re-evaluated for exclusion and referral to abstinence-orientated treatment.

Program Content

Modifications of the ASTP. Feedback from participants of Study I indicated that the most useful aspects of the program were self-monitoring of drinking behavior and knowledge of blood alcohol levels. This self-report feedback from the first study made practical sense: isolated and brief interventions relating to broader lifestyle issues seemed less relevant to a group of young persons who do not see alcohol as a primary problem in their lives. Rather, direct and specific knowledge about personal drinking habits, alcohol effects, and skills to use in this regard can more easily be accepted and practiced.

We chose to organize intervention content around two key assumptions: (1) alcohol consumer at moderate blood alcohol levels (BAL < 0.05%) significantly reduces the risk of accidents, illness, embarrassment, hangovers, etc.; and (2) alcohol effects in social settings are largely dependent on expectancies or beliefs about these effects, and *not* on the pharmacological properties of alcohol. These two central themes were repeated frequently as they were applied to common 'high-risk' situations in which alcohol is typically consumed by college students. Issues of broader lifestyle management were included but de-emphasized compared to the first study.

In our revised intervention, we presented information on BAL monitoring and limit-setting early in the program (sessions 1 and 2). The placebo drinking experience was included in session 2, much earlier in the program than in the first study. After these initial presentations, experiences with limit-setting (both successful and unsuccessful) in specific situations became the central context of program discussions. Emphasizing a situational approach, we explored common expectations, motives, and coping strategies.

Session 3 was organized around positive affect social occasions (parties), and common beliefs about the power of alcohol to create a good time. Session 4 focused more on uncomfortable social situations, those in which students feel insecure and/or out of place. The power of alcohol to become 'liquid courage' was challenged, as was the social influence of their 'drinking buddies.' Principles of assertive behavior as an introduction to the skill of refusing drinks were reviewed. Session 5 was oriented toward experiences of negative affect that were not necessarily social in nature. Students were reminded of the temporary nature of alcohol's pleasant effects and the long-term nature of alcohol's negative effects. Session 6 was a summary of the program, and included suggestions for maintaining program gains.

In each session, students were asked, after increasing their awareness by drinking placebos and monitoring their own drinking, whether they believed alcohol chemically provided the desired effects. They were challenged to test whether enjoyment was possible at lower BAL levels or without drinking altogether.

A workbook paralleled the subject content of the revised ASTP. In the classroom, this workbook was used as a supplement to presentations and discussions; in the correspondence course, it served as the self-help manual.

Classroom Format. Approximately eight subjects were assigned per group, assignments being based on meeting availability. An effort was made to evenly distribute males and females, as well as students in various years of study. Subjects in the classroom condition attended six weekly ninety-minute meetings led by a male and female co-therapy team. The group meetings consisted of presentations and demonstrations by the group leaders, and a discussion of the program content. The second classroom meeting was held in a simulated bar in which placebo drinks were provided, as described in Study 1. Subjects were given one section of the workbook each week and asked to turn in homework assignments at the beginning of the next session.

Correspondence Format. Subjects assigned to the Correspondence Format were asked to complete six units over the same six-week period as the classroom meetings. Each correspondence unit averaged seventeen pages, including graphs and diagrams of important points. Each unit contained a review of the previous unit's homework assignment, some "New Ideas" for the week, some "Exercises" to elaborate program points (e.g., an expectancy questionnaire; assertive drink refusals), and a homework assignment for the following week. Students were asked to complete approximately one unit per week, and to turn in their homework assignments when completed.

Professional Advice Format. Subjects assigned to the Professional Advice condition completed all assessment procedures but did not receive the six-session (or unit) skills training program. Instead, these subjects completed a one-hour, individual interview with a program staff member. In the interview, each subject's assessment was reviewed, and recommendations for reducing risk were provided. Interviewers followed a prescribed outline emphasizing the central points of the ASTP. Subjects were given a BAL monitoring card and taught basic aspects of BAL calculation. Beliefs about alcohol effects were questioned through a brief description of research with the balanced placebo design. Limit-setting was introduced, and students were encouraged to make changes in their drinking patterns. Students were given a written copy of the program recommendations.

Subjects in Study II

The sample of 134 individuals who completed the program is 52 percent female, and averages twenty-one (SD = 3.58) years of age. Although the sample is slightly younger than that of the first study, patterns of drinking are quite similar. Examination of drinking assessments revealed that 24 percent reported parental history of alcohol problems and MAST scores averaged 6.08. Based on interview retrospective reports, subjects consumed an average of 19.75 drinks per week on 3.79 drinking occasions, an average of over five drinks per drinking day. Estimated peak BAL for these retrospective reports of weekly drinking averaged 0.14 percent.

Results of Study II

Initially, there was considerable difficulty getting students assigned to the correspondence condition to complete reading and writing assignments. Only 13 of 30 (43%) of subjects completed all assignments. Eight individuals completed no assignments at all. Also, individuals in the correspondence condition were quite likely to drop out of the study altogether: 30 percent by post-treatment assessment, and 63 percent by the three-month assessment. As a result of this high attrition rate, the correspondence condition was dropped midway through the study. Data obtained from those who completed correspondence materials indicated comparable drinking reductions to those of subjects in the Classroom and Professional Advice conditions. Nevertheless, our difficulty in administering the correspondence course suggests that reading materials alone are unlikely to be an effective means of altering most students' drinking habits. Subsequent analyses include only the Classroom and Professional Advice conditions.

Data from student evaluations of the Classroom and Professional Advice programs again show the ASTP to be understandable and helpful to students once they decide to participate. The classroom condition was clearly best liked among the groups and rated higher for assistance in changing drinking when assessed post-treatment ($\overline{X}$ = 5.16 for Classroom vs $\overline{X}$ = 3.83 for Advice, on a 7-point scale, $F(1, 40) = 9.73$, $p < .003$). Students also reported that they were more likely to recommend the classroom program to others ($\overline{X}$ = 6.00 for Classroom vs $\overline{X}$ = 4.74 for Advice on a 7 = point scale, $F(1, 40) = 7.65$, $p < .009$).

As in the first study, all subjects significantly reduced their alcohol consumption during the course of the six-week program. Changes in drinking were quite similar to those found in Study I. For those providing post-treatment data, average SECs reduced from 12.46 (SD = 7.8) pre-treatment to 8.46 (SD = 6.4) post-treatment ($F(1,78) = 24.1$, $p < .001$). PBAL declined in similar manner, 0.14 percent (SD = 0.09) to 0.10 percent (SD = 0.08) ($F(1,79) = 16.25$, $p < .001$).

Figure 2 shows the decline in SECs and PBAL separately for the two treatment groups through a two-year follow-up period. Non-significant repeated measures (ANOVAs) for the post-treatment and follow-up assessments indicate that reductions in drinking are generally maintained. At each assessment, subjects in the classroom condition drink least, although differences between the conditions only approach statistical significance.

It is noteworthy that the Professional Advice Format was easier to complete than the Classroom Format, yet tentatively shows comparable treatment effectiveness to that of the classroom intervention. Although these data are preliminary, a careful individual assessment, followed by specific advice and recommendations for drinking reductions, may prove to be an efficient intervention for college students.

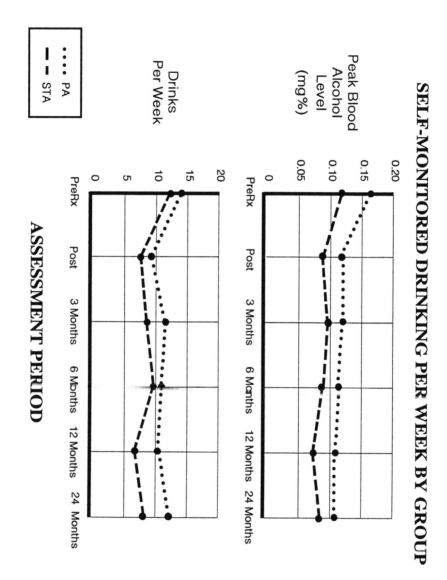

SELF-MONITORED DRINKING PER WEEK BY GROUP

ASSESSMENT PERIOD

Clinical Issues with College Student Populations

The research programs described here have involved careful consideration of the style and technique of presenting students with suggestions and skills for changing their drinking and social behavior. Although not a central component of our research design, the importance of clinical issues should not be overlooked. The best program content can have little effect if presented in a manner that students perceive as 'not relevant' or 'too rigid.' From the opposite end of the continuum, the broader alcohol treatment community has sometimes misperceived our work as promoting drinking. Below are some of the community and clinical issues we have had to address in developing a risk-reduction program with populations of student drinkers.

Ethics of a Risk-reduction Program. Administering a program that seeks to reduce rather than eliminate risk involves careful attention to professional and community ethics. From a public health perspective, risk-reduction is a key goal. Some members of the addiction treatment community may object to our work, however, contending that, by not supporting abstinence, we are giving underage students (and students with drinking problems) 'permission' to drink. We contend that it is inappropriate to rigidly support abstinence goals that students will not accept. Furthermore, most students who abuse alcohol do not meet criteria for physical dependency, and will continue to drink regardless of the program message. We carefully screen out individuals showing signs of alcohol dependence and refer them to abstinence-oriented treatment. Perhaps most importantly, students are challenged to consider if drinking is necessary. In fact, students are not required to drink in the ASTP; several have chosen to abstain from all drinking. An additional message of the ASTP is that failure at risk-reduction is a good indication that abstinence is the most appropriate goal.

Motivation. It is axiomatic that individuals need to be motivated to be successful in changing behavior. Treatment of addictive problems presents a particularly difficult example of confused and/or ambivalent motivations. Miller (1983) has thoughtfully elaborated on the basic ambivalence of persons with drinking problems: they want to drink, yet do not want to experience the negative consequences associated with drinking. In work with college students, problems with ambivalent motivations are compounded. Specifically, students are unlikely to report concern about their drinking. Instead, they are typically motivated by curiosity, concern because of family history, or some mild anxiety that their drinking may some day develop into a problem. To complicate matters, these individuals generally enjoy drinking. Alcohol is a central aspect of most college social occasions, and represents one of the few 'adult' activities that college students can participate in.

Interventions with college students, then, must not exacerbate ambivalence, but be framed in a style that assists young adults to personally evaluate their lifestyles. For persons at an early age who have experienced few problems, confrontational communication seldom promotes risk reduction (cf. Miller, 1983). Persons told they have 'a problem' are likely to become defensive, and to argue that this is not true.

Our skills training program attempts to help subjects define for themselves both desirable and undesirable consequences of drinking. Students are asked how they would recognize a drinking problem if one should arise in the future. The immediate negative consequences of drinking (e.g., hangovers, social embarrassment, lack of money) are emphasized in addition to long-term risks. Class leaders encourage students to evaluate the pros and cons of heavy drinking, and to 'experiment' with alternatives. For example, we often ask students to define how they decide to stop drinking (when nauseous? when the keg is dry?). We then suggest a strategy of stopping at a moderate BAL: when risks are minimal. We label this the 'point of diminishing returns.' In essence, students are challenged to drink moderately, not out of fear of negative consequences, but out of an effort to enjoy themselves in a less risky fashion.

Affect. Students seldom acknowledge that alcohol is significantly involved with affective states other than celebrations and parties (Brennan, Walfish, & Aubuchon, 1986). Negative affect drinking is often seen as the result of alcohol dependence, rather than its cause (Cox, 1987). In addition, students do not perceive heavy drinking as a failure of personal control, and are not emotionally invested in making changes. To communicate better with students, we have chosen to frame many of our interventions in cognitive—and less emotional—terms.

As was noted earlier, the central components of the program are knowledge about psychological and social effects of alcohol, and strategies for managing specific, often high-risk, situations. The Goal Violation Effect is an hypothesized pattern of responding to lapses in planned behavior changes, e.g., exceeding planned drinking limits (Marlatt & Gordon, 1985). This pattern is usually described as feelings of guilt and remorse, a loss in self-confidence, and a self-attribution of lack of control. For working with college student drinkers, we suggest that a lapse will likely seem to be incongruent with the previous goal, to cause people to question their motivation and desire, and to change their goals. We then explain that one lapse can be experienced as a learning experience, and does not indicate a permanent change in attitude or goals.

Future Directions for Research

Further refinement of the skills training approach with college students can proceed in a number of directions. First, increased acceptance and participation remains a challenge. It is noteworthy that students will not usually volunteer purely for the learning experience; although once involved, they enjoy and benefit from the program. Perhaps students need to be compensated in some other form for taking extra time for learning about risk-reduction (e.g., receiving class credit). Second, measurements for assessing change in behavior and attitudes are weak. Although we infer that we are able to change understanding of alcohol effects, we have, as yet, been unsuccessful in measuring such changes (Fromme, Kivlahan, &

Marlatt, 1986). Third, more efficient professional efforts may be produced by selecting participants who are most likely to benefit from a skills training approach during the college years. Our current data suggest that modest improvements are possible for some well-motivated individuals. We plan a number of analyses aimed at identifying those who respond best to the program. Finally, because so much college student drinking occurs in the context of well-defined social organizations (i.e., dormitory floors, fraternities, and sororities), drinking interventions may be most effective when targeted and administered to entire social groups.

College student drinking is a complex behavior with many associated causal factors. Our experience (and much research) with these populations suggests that one-dimensional programs based on fear of future problems such as developing alcoholism are minimally effective. Similarly, programs based on only one aspect of college life (i.e., drinking) are too narrow. College student drinkers represent a unique group for early intervention and prevention efforts. Special treatment and referral programs should be established for students who show signs of advanced alcohol dependency and require an abstinence goal, but most students could benefit from a risk-reduction approach. We now feel that we have a reasonable technology for changing student drinking. As in many other prevention programs, we are left with the challenge of finding and/or motivating individuals to use the available tools.

Acknowledgments

This research was supported by National Institute on Alcohol Abuse and Alcoholism grant #2 R01 AA05591–04 to G. Alan Marlatt. We express our sincere appreciation to Don Wood for editorial assistance, Jewel Brien for graphics, and Susan Tapert for technical assistance in the preparation of this chapter.

Parts reprinted from Heather, Miller, & Greeley, *Self-control and the addictive behaviours* (Botany, NSW: Maxwell MacMillan) by permission of publisher.

References

Alden, L. E. (1988). Behavioral self-management controlled drinking strategies in a context of secondary prevention. *Journal of Consulting and Clinical Psychology, 56,* 280–286.

Baer, J. S., Marlatt, G. A., Kivlahan, D. R., Fromme, K., Larimer, M. E., & Williams, E. (1992). An experimental test of three methods of alcohol risk reduction with young adults. *Journal of Consulting and Clinical Psychology, 60* (6), 974-979.

Berkowitz, A. D., & Perkins, H. W. (1986). Problem drinking among college students: A review of recent research. *Journal of American College Health, 35,* 21–28.

Brennan, A. F., Walfish, S., & Aubuchon, P. (1986). Problem drinking among college students: A review of recent research. *Journal of American College Health, 35,* 21–28.

Cahalan, D., & Room, R. (1974). *Problem drinking among American men.* New Brunswick, N.J.: Center of Alcohol Studies, Rutgers University.

Chaney, E. F., O'Leary, M. R., & Marlatt, G. A. (1978). Skill training with alcoholics. *Journal of Consulting and Clinical Psychology, 46,* 1092–1104.

Collins, R. L., & Marlatt, G. A. (1981). Social modeling as a determinant of drinking behavior: Implications for prevention and treatment. *Addictive Behaviors, 6,* 233–240.

Cox, W. M. (1987). Personality theory and research. In H. T. Blaine & K. E. Leonard (Eds.), *Psychological theories of drinking and alcoholism.* New York: Guilford Press.

Critchlow, B. (1986). The power of John Barleycorn: Beliefs about the effects of alcohol on social behavior. *American Psychologist, 41,* 751–764.

Fillmore, K. M. (1987). Prevalence, incidence and chronicity of drinking patterns and problems among men as a function of age: A longitudinal and cohort analysis. *British Journal of Addiction, 82,* 77–83.

Fillmore, K. M., Bacon, S., & Hyman, M. (1979). *The 27 year longitudinal panel study of drinking by students in college, 1949–1976. Final report to NIAAA* (Contract no. ADM281–76–0015). Rockville, Md.: NIAAA.

Fillmore, K. M., & Midanik, L. (1984). Chronicity of drinking problems among men: A longitudinal study. *Journal of Studies on Alcohol, 45,* 228–236.

Fromme, K., Kivlahan, D. R., & Marlatt, G. A. (1986). Alcohol expectancies, risk identification, and secondary prevention with problem drinkers. *Advances in Behavior Research and Therapy, 8,* 237–251.

Gonzalez, G. M. (1981). *The BACCHUS handbook.* Gainesville, Fla.: University of Florida Campus Alcohol Information Center.

Goodstadt, M.S. (1986). Alcohol education research and practice: A logical analysis of the two realities. *Journal of Drug Education, 16,* 349–365.

Goodstadt, M. S., & Caleekal-John, A. (1984). Alcohol education programs for university students: A review of their effectiveness. *The International Journal of the Addictions, 19,* 721–741.

Hay, W. M., & Nathan, P. E. (1982). *Clinical case studies in the behavioral treatment of alcoholism.* New York: Plenum Press.

Heather, N., Whitton, B., & Robertson, I. (1986). Evaluation of a self-help manual for media-recruited problem drinkers: Six-month follow-up results. *British Journal of Clinical Psychology, 25,* 19–34.

Horn, J. L., Skinner, H. A., Wanberg, K., & Foster, F. M. (1984). *Alcohol use questionnaire (ADS).* Toronto: Addiction Research Foundation.

Institute of Medicine (1990). *Broadening the base of treatment for alcohol problems,* Washington, D.C.: National Academy Press.

Kivlahan, D. R., Marlatt, G. A., Fromme, K., Coppel, D. B., & Williams, E. (1990. Secondary prevention with college drinkers: Evaluation of an alcohol skills training program. *Journal of Consulting and Clinical Psychology 58* (6), 805–810.

Kraft, D. P. (1984). A comprehensive prevention program for college students. In P. M. Miller & T. D. Nirenberg (Eds.), *Prevention of alcohol abuse.* New York: Plenum Press.

Lang, A. R., & Marlatt, G. A. (1983). Problem drinking: A social learning perspective. In R. J. Gatchel, A. Baum, & J. E. Singer (Eds.), *Handbook of psychology and health: Vol. 1: Clinical psychology and behavioral medicine: Overlapping disciplines.* Hillsdale, N.J.: Lawrence Erlbaum Press.

Marlatt, G. A. (1987). Alcohol, the magic elixir: Stress, expectancy, and the transformation of emotional states. In E. Gottheil, K. A. Druly, S. Pashko, & S. P. Weinstein (Eds.), *Stress and addiction*. New York: Brunner/Mazel.

Marlatt, G. A., & Gordon, J. R. (Eds.). (1985). *Relapse prevention: Maintenance strategies in the treatment of addictive behaviors.* New York: Guilford Press.

Marlatt, G. A., & Miller, W. R. (1984). *Comprehensive drinker profile.* Odessa, Fla.: Psychological Assessment Resources, Inc.

Marlatt, G. A., & Nathan, P. E. (1978). *Behavioral approaches to alcoholism*. New Brunswick, N.J.: Center of Alcohol Studies, Rutgers University.

Mathews, D. B., & Miller, W. R. (1979). Estimating blood alcohol concentrations: Two computer programs and their applictions in therapy and research. *Addictive Behaviors, 4,* 55–60.

Mauss, A. L., Hopkins, R. H., Weisheit, R. A., & Kearney, K. A. (1988). The problematic prospects for prevention in the classroom: Should alcohol education programs be expected to reduce drinking by youth? *Journal of Studies on Alcohol, 49,* 51–61.

Miller, P. M. (1976). *Behavioral treatment of alcoholism*. Oxford: Pergamon Press.

Miller, W. R. (1983). Motivational interviewing with problem drinkers. *Behavioral Psychotherapy, 11,* 147–172.

Miller, W. R., & Hester, R. K. (1986). Inpatient alcoholism treatment: Who benefits? *American Psychologist, 41,* 794–805.

Miller, W. R., & Taylor, C. A. (1980). Relative effectiveness of bibliotherapy, individual and group self-control training in the treatment of problem drinkers. *Addictive Behaviors, 5,* 13–24.

Mills, K. C., & McCarty, D. (1983). A data based alcohol abuse prevention program in a university setting. *Journal of Alcohol and Drug Education, 28,* 115–27.

Moskowitz, J. M. (1989). The primary prevention of alcohol problems: A critical review of the research literature. *Journal of Studies on Alcohol, 50,* 54–88.

Murphy, T. J., Pagano, R. R., & Marlatt, G. A. (1986). Lifestyle modification with heavy alcohol drinkers: Effects of aerobic exercise and meditation. *Addictive Behaviors, 11,* 175–186.

NIAAA. (1984). *Report of the 1983 Prevention Planning Panel.* Rockville, Md.: NIAAA.

Orford, J., & Edwards, G. (1977). *Alcoholism: A comparison of treatment and advice, with a study of the influence of marriage.* New York: Oxford University Press.

Rozelle, G. R. (1980). Experiential and cognitive small group approaches to alcohol education for college students. *Journal of Alcohol and Drug Education, 26,* 40–54.

Saltz, R., & Elandt, D. (1986). College student drinking studies 1976–1985. *Contemporary Drug Problems,* Spring, 117–119.

Sancehez-Craig, M., Annis, H. M., Bornet, A. R., & MacDonald, K. R. (1984). Random assignment to abstinence and controlled drinking: Evaluation of a cognitive-behavioral program for problem drinkers. *Journal of Consulting and Clinical Psychology, 52,* 390–403.

Selzer, M. L. (1971). The Michigan Alcoholism Screening Test: The quest for a new diagnostic instrument. *American Journal of Psychiatry, 127,* 1653–1658.

Sherwood, J. S. (Ed.). (1987). *Alcohol policies and practices on college and university campuses.* New York: National Association of Student Personnel Administrators.

Walfish, S., Wentz, D., Benzing, P, Brennan, F., & Champ, S. (1981). Alcohol abuse on a college campus: A needs assessment. *Evaluation and Program Planning, 4,* 163–168.

SPIRITUALITY IN TREATMENT
AND RECOVERY

John E. Keller

In addressing spirituality in the treatment of and recovery from alcoholism, it is important to address what happened in regard to science, psychiatry, psychology and religion. For almost forty years, the primary focus for recovery in most professional treatment programs has been the spiritual recovery program in the fellowship of Alcoholics Anonymous which was founded in 1935. Clearly there can be the appearance of something very problematic in identifying alcoholism as a chronic progressive disease for which the best treatment and sustained recovery has a primary focus on a spiritual way of life within a self-help group. It is also interesting to note that the alcoholism treatment field has done an effective job of integrating this spiritual dimension. But the field has some real catch-up work to do in fully integrating the medical, psycho-social aspects of the process into appropriate, comprehensive, levels of the service system required for any chronic progressive disease. This approach is quite different from what has been the approach historically, and what has occurred in the recent history of treatment of other chronic diseases.

For some years after Alcoholics Anonymous came into being, most psychiatrists and psychologists ignored it, discounted it, or were baffled by it. These professionals were put off by that "admitting powerlessness over alcohol," "coming to believe in a power greater than ourselves," "turning your life over to the care of God as you understood him," "moral inventory," "meditation and prayer and seeking God's will," "spiritual awakening and carrying the message to others."

Most helping professionals who did take a look, did so

from a detached—even aloof—position, through their own biases, preconceptions, and belief systems. Adopting a self-fulfilling prophecy approach, they never did go into the fellowship to take people seriously, to see what they might learn from them, their experiences and their language. Professionals remained convinced that the drinking was simply symptomatic of an underlying serious psychiatric or psychological disorder.

In the United States, the first major scientific, medical, and psycho-social thrust came with the founding of the Yale Center of Alcohol Studies (now at Rutgers University) in 1940. (The Center was not officially named until 1943). The focus was on getting past the "wet-dry" controversy and moving to the establishment and dissemination of the scientific facts on alcohol, alcohol use, alcohol problems, and alcoholism. It is both important and interesting to note that the group of scientists who headed up this endeavor decided early on to include on their staff a non-scientist, recovering alcoholic (Lefty) who was knowledgeable of (and active in) the spiritual recovery program of Alcoholics Anonymous. Somehow they sensed or knew that such a presence was not only necessary but also desirable in their endeavors.

In the Yale Summer School of Alcohol Studies programs, after a series of lectures by the faculty on the scientific facts, Lefty was introduced for his presentation. With a clear sense of honest respect and value for the scientists and the scientific approach, and with a delightful sense of humor, he shared the "unscientific story" of his active alcoholism and then recovery in Alcoholics Anonymous through the Twelve Step spiritual recovery program. He used words like "surrender," "higher power," "faith," "will of God," "prayer," "meditation," and "spiritual awakening." Doing so was not only fine with the scientific leadership people, it was exactly what they wanted from him. The recovering people in Alcoholics Anonymous who attended the summer school had problems with the scientists and their language. But participants were encouraged that these scientists were addressing alcoholism as a disease that needed direct treatment, rather than simply being symptomatic of an underlying disorder. It is also interesting and important to note that when Lefty's scientist colleagues spoke or wrote on alcoholism—the disease concept, its etiology, progression, treatment, and recovery, and the significance of Alcoholics Anonymous—they never used spiritual terminology. Scientists used medical and psychosocial terminology and still referenced Alcoholics Anonymous as being a social reality. The assumption that spiritual and scientific didn't and couldn't mix was honored—even though these different approaches were clearly mixed in the staffing of the Center. Even if they could be mixed, the scientists didn't know how (or didn't feel comfortable and free) to use spiritual language. But scientists did assure that someone would be on the staff who could articulate the spiritual recovery program of Alcoholics Anonymous.

Today there are numerous physicians, psychiatrists, psychologists, and social workers, as well as some scientific researchers, who have learned that there can be an integration of the scientific and the spiritual in their life and scientific pursuit. For some it has come in their own recovery through the spiritual program of Alcoholics Anonymous. One of the co-founders of Alcoholics Anonymous was a physician.

The Beginnings of Alcoholics Anonymous

Bill Wilson and Dr. Bob Smith were the co-founders of Alcoholics Anonymous. An old school friend of Bill Wilson named Ebby was an alcoholic. Bill had heard that Ebby was going to be committed for alcoholic insanity. One day Ebby called Bill. He was sober. Ebby came to see Bill, who was drinking. He spoke of having found help through religion. Ebby had gotten involved with the religious Oxford Groups.

> Ebby told Bill that the group told him he had to admit that he was licked. He also said: I learned that I ought to take stock of myself and confess my defects to another person in confidence; I

learned that I needed to make restitution for the harm I had done others. I was told that I ought to practice the kind of giving that has no price tag on it, the giving of yourself to somebody. Now, he added, I know you are going to gag on this, but they taught me that I should try to pray to whatever God I thought there was for the power to carry out these simple precepts. And if I did not believe there was any God, then I had better try the experiment of praying to whatever God there might be. And you know, Bill, it's a queer thing, but even before I had done all this, just as soon as I decided that I would try with an open mind, it seemed to me that my drinking problem was lifted right out of me. It wasn't like the water wagon business at all. This time I felt completely released of the desire, and I have not had a drink for months.

Ebby didn't try to pressure or evangelize me, and pretty soon he left. For several days I went on drinking. But in no waking hour was the thought of my friend absent from my mind. I could not forget what he had said. In the kinship of common suffering, one alcoholic had been talking to another. (Wilson, 1939, pp. 58–59)

Bill was under the care of Dr. William D. Silkworth, who had a theory that alcoholism had two components. The first was an obsession that compelled the sufferer to drink against his will and the second was some metabolic difficulty which Silkworth called an allergy. The obsession caused the alcoholic to continue drinking and the allergy caused the sufferer to deteriorate, go insane or die. Although Silkworth had initially thought Bill could be helped, he finally told Bill that his case was hopeless. This was a shattering blow. Hospitalized once more, and clear of alcohol, Bill was terribly depressed. In anguish he finally cried out, "If there is a God, let Him show Himself! I am ready to do anything, anything!"

Suddenly the room lit up with a great white light. I was caught up into an ecstasy which there are no words to describe. It seemed to me, in the mind's eye, that I was on a mountain and that a wind not of air but of spirit was blowing. And then it burst upon me that I was a free man. Slowly the ecstasy subsided. I lay on the bed, but now for a time I was in another world, a new world of consciousness. All about me and through me there was a wonderful feeling of Presence, and I thought to myself, So this is the God of the preachers! A great peace stole over me and I thought, No matter how wrong things seem to be, they are still all right. Things are all right with God and His world.

Then, little by little, I began to be frightened. My modern education crawled back and said to me, You are hallucinating. You had better get the doctor. Dr. Silkworth asked me a lot of questions. After a while he said, No, Bill, you are not crazy. There has been some basic psychological or spiritual event here. I've read about these things in the books. Sometimes spiritual experiences do release people from alcoholism. Immensely relieved, I fell again to wondering what actually had happened.

More light on this came the next day. It was Ebby, I think, who brought me a copy of William James' *Varieties of Religious Experience*. It was rather difficult reading for me, but I devoured it from cover to cover. Spiritual experiences, James thought, could have objective reality; almost like gifts from the blue, they could transform people. Some were sudden brilliant illumina-tions; others came on very gradually. Some flowed out of religious channels; others did not. But nearly all had the great common denomin-

ators of pain, suffering, calamity. Complete hopelessness and deflation at depth were almost
always required to make the recipient ready. The
significance of all this burst upon me. Deflation
at depth—yes, that was it. Exactly that had happened to me. Dr. Carl Jung had told an Oxford
group friend of Ebby's how hopeless his alcoholism was and Dr. Silkworth had passed the
same sentence upon me. (Wilson, 1939, pp. 63–
64)

There was an even earlier link in the chain of events that
led to the founding of Alcoholics Anonymous. In the January
1963 issue of the *A.A. Grapevine* magazine, the correspondence
between Bill Wilson and Dr. Carl Jung of Zurich was published.
In 1961, Bill wrote Jung explaining how the doctor had influenced
a patient, Roland H., during the 1930s.

Roland H. greatly admired Dr. Jung, but after leaving his
care relapsed into intoxication. He returned to Jung, who told
him frankly of the hopelessness of his case as far as medical or
psychiatric treatment might help. When Roland asked if there
might be any other hope, Jung said that although very rare,
sometimes a spiritual or religious experience—a genuine conversion—might work. He advised Roland to place himself in a
religious atmosphere and hope for the best. Roland then joined
the Oxford Groups and did find a conversion experience that
released him from his complusion to drink. Returning to New
York, Roland worked with Dr. Samuel Shoemaker in the
Oxford Groups, and was the one who brought the message to
Ebby.

Carl Jung sent the following letter in reply.

Dear Mr. W.,
Your letter has been very welcome indeed. I had
no news from Roland H. anymore and often
wondered what has been his fate. Our conversation which he has adequately reported to

you had an aspect of which he did not know. The reason that I could not tell him everything was that those days I had to be exceedingly careful of what I said. I found out that I was misunderstood in every possible way. Thus I was very careful when I talked to Roland H. But what I really thought about, was the result of many experiences with men of his kind. His craving for alcohol was the equivalent, on a low level, of the spiritual thirst of our being for wholeness, expressed in medieval language: the union with God. "As the heart panteth after the water brooks, so panteth my soul after thee, O God." (Psalm 42, 1)

How could one formulate such an insight in a language that is not misunderstood in our days? The only right and legitimate way to such an experience is, that it happens to you when you walk on a path which leads you to higher understanding. You might be led to that goal by an act of grace or through a personal and honest contact with friends, or through a higher education of the mind beyond the confines of mere rationalism. I see from your letter that Roland H. has chosen the second way, which was, under the circumstances, obviously the best one.

I am strongly convinced that the evil principle prevailing in this world leads the unrecognized spiritual need into perdition, if it is not counteracted either by real religious insight or by the protective wall of human community. An ordinary man, not protected by an action from above and isolated in society, cannot resist the power of evil, which is called very aptly the Devil. But the use of such words arouses so many mistakes that one can only keep aloof from them as much as possible.

These are the reasons why I could not give a

full and sufficient explanation to Roland H. but I am risking it with you because I conclude from your very decent and honest letter that you have acquired a point of view above the misleading platitudes one usually hears about alcoholism.

You see, Alcohol in Latin is "spiritus" and you use the same word for the highest religious experience as well as for the most depraving poison. The helpful formula therefore is: SPIRITUS CONTRA SPIRITUM.

Thanking you again for your kind letter. I remain yours sincerely,

C. G. Jung

Alcoholics Anonymous and the Church

The Oxford Groups had four moral absolutes: absolute honesty, absolute purity, absolute unselfishness, and absolute love. Also included was "getting down on your knees" when asking God to remove all shortcomings. Clearly there is no human capable of attaining those four absolutes. Interestingly and importantly, they were not incorporated into the formulation of the Twelve Steps of Alcoholics Anonymous, nor was the phrase "on your knees." It was the consensus of the group that all of that would be too much for many alcoholics and might scare them away.

When the recovering people began to pool their common experiences—which became the Twelve Steps of Alcoholics Anonymous—they had great difficulty with God terminology. An Episcopalian minister's son wanted the steps to be Christian in the doctrinal sense, using biblical terms and expressions. According to Bill Wilson, the atheists and agnostics didn't want the word "God" used. The group finally settled on the phrase "power greater than ourselves." Bill claimed this represented a great contribution by the atheists and agnostics because it left the door open for alcoholics wanting sobriety to perceive in any way that made sense to them. It was believed that regardless of the way newcomers perceived, believed, and talked about the higher power, most would in time come to call that power God.

It is interesting to note that once the group decided on "power greater than ourselves," the word "God" was used in the rest of the steps. One explanation might be that once they dispensed with the moralistic, judgmental perception of God by exploring the phrase "power greater than ourselves," they had no trouble using the name "God" in the rest of the steps. God's name apparently then became a good name for all.

One might expect that since Alcoholics Anonymous was a spiritual recovery program, it would be less problematic for the church than it had been for science. This wasn't the case, despite the influence of individual clergy. Early in the history Dr. Samuel Shoemaker, an Episcopalian priest, and Father Edward Dowling, a Jesuit, were very influential and highly valued (Wilson, 1939). Other members of the clergy who became familiar with Alcoholics Anonymous and encouraged alcoholics to go to their meetings were typically appreciated within the local group. But, on the whole, Alcoholics Anonymous was problematic for most Christian clergy. (There were very few if any Jewish alcoholics in the early days.)

One of the problems for the church was that Alcoholics Anonymous was seen as a religion—and a non-Christian religion—because it used the words "higher power" and "God," but not the name of Jesus Christ. Moreover, most of those who got sober in this so-called "spiritual program" didn't go to church, while a significant number of those who continued to seek help in their religion continued to drink. But the major problem was the moralistic, judgmental attitude and response that the church, like society, had toward alcoholics. Their drinking was seen only as sin, and alcoholics were perceived to be among the "chief of sinners." Indeed they were often moral outcasts. Thus the concept of alcoholism as an illness or disease was problematic, along with the phenomena that alcoholics were recovering in a non-church fellowship with a spiritual recovery program. Further, these sober "drunkards" swore a lot and that meant they really weren't sincere—no matter how much they talked about their recovery being by the grace of God.

What Alcoholics Anonymous calls a spiritual recovery program is clearly also a very moral program. The church needed to learn that there is a tremendous difference between moralism and morality.

Moralism is not only an attitude but also results in behaviors. It is conditional and judgmental. Moralism attaches strings to acceptance, so it is, in fact, nonacceptance. Moralism is seeing oneself as being more righteous than another person. It is not only the rejection of unacceptable behavior, such as the behavior of alcoholism, but it is rejection of the person in whose life the behavior exists.

Moralism is proscriptive (i.e., "shouldn't-ism"): "You shouldn't be like that. You shouldn't do that. You shouldn't have done that. You shouldn't feel that way." Or, "I shouldn't be like that. I shouldn't do that. I shouldn't have done that. I shouldn't feel that way."

Although "shouldn't-ism" looks like evidence that a person wants to change negative realities in his or her life, the A.A. paradigm assures us that change won't occur. As long as alcoholics moralize, the drinking will continue. I feel that is true with all human problems where change is needed. Try to identify any basic negative reality in your life that was changed as a result of "shouldn'tism!" This is because moralistic proscription is nonacceptance. By contrast, seeing alcoholism as an illness helps alcoholics to end the moralizing that blocks acceptance of their human limitation. When the moralism goes, and the person can say, "This is me and my condition, and I want to change," change can occur. This is a reality we can observe in our personal living.

Morality recognizes that there is a moral law in and about life that has to do with God, self, and others and that has within it personal as well as societal responsibility and accountability.

The words "church," "religion," "God," "Jesus Christ "were filled with moralism in the experience and minds of alcoholics. Added to this problem is the fact that no matter how moralistic the church had been, alcoholics are equally moralistic with themselves about their condition. There is a tremendous sense of guilt and shame together with self-condemnation (Kurtz, 1980). That there could be love and acceptance for them, which indeed they needed in order to experience help and hope, was beyond the comprehension of many alcoholics.

Once alcoholics find and experience understanding and love, they are able to believe in and live a spiritual-moral way of life for recovery which they can follow in the Twelve Steps. Clearly in those steps alcoholics recognize and accept, not only their need for God's help and presence in their lives, but also their need to accept the moral responsibility and accountability for their own feelings, attitudes, and behaviors. And with that they gain the wisdom to know and believe that such spiritual change and growth can only be a reality if there is involvement with and caring for others.

Except for some "fundamentalist expressions" the church today has generally come to understand and accept Alcoholics Anonymous as a needed and effective spiritual recovery program. Many clergy are recovering members of the fellowship. Congregations provide meeting rooms and often develop ministry support teams for raising the levels of understanding on alcoholism and Alcoholics Anonymous, as well as serving as referral resources.

Surrender

In 1955, I was asked to go to Willmar State Hospital, Willmar, Minnesota, to the state treatment program for alcoholics. At that time, the staff was putting together what became the model for modern alcoholism treatment. I was told to stay there until I thought I knew something significant to share with the church. I was told to get extensive exposure to Alcoholics Anonymous by going to numerous meetings, talking with recovering people in that fellowship, and reading their literature.

Only after much extensive exposure and direct involvement with patients and recovering alcoholics did it become clear that alcoholism is "powerlessness over alcohol." It became clear, at least for me, that the struggle in the professional treatment and scientific communities with that statement was not essentially a professional struggle (for the professional treatment person, including clinically trained clergy) nor a scientific struggle (for the behaviorial scientists.) Rather it involved a basic human struggle with becoming aware of and accepting what Ernest Kurtz identifies as "essential human limitation," particularly in one's own life. The professional treatment staff and research staff at Willmar had come to understand and accept that this first step in the Alcoholics Anonymous program is basic. There are still many professional clinicians who believe that "essential human limitation" is an inappropriate focus if a person is going to do anything about a human problem. Such individuals might claim that the focus needs to be on human potential. In Alcoholics Anonymous there is wisdom in understanding that to not begin with step one means to not begin with the reality of the disease of alcoholism, and that often means no beginning for people afflicted with this disease.

Early in the development of Alcoholics Anonymous, Dr. Harry Tiebout, a psychoanalyst, became involved and made a great contribution in helping us to understand some of the basic questions and dynamics of this recovery program. Having applied analytic concepts, approaches, and experience to the treatment of alcoholism patients, he completely failed to help them recover. He could have responded by saying that they really did not want to quit drinking and get well, but he didn't because he was convinced that many of them did want to quit. Rather, he decided that there was something he didn't yet understand. So, in the midst of his failure, he decided to stay with the patients' experience and listened carefully to what they were saying.

As he stayed with them, one of his patients quit drinking and began to recover. Not only had she quit drinking, but there was clinical evidence of a basic inner change which was reflected in her attitudes and behavior. Since Tiebout had no explanation for her recovery, he asked the patient if she would help him understand what had happened. She said that she had "surrendered." That concept had little meaning in his psychiatric frame of understanding, but he took her seriously. He asked her to write

how she felt before and after this phenomenon. What she wrote
was exactly what he had observed:

Before I felt...	*After I feel...*
unstable	at peace
tense	safe
nervous	composed
afraid	relaxed
guilty	contented
ashamed	thankful
pushed	cleansed
incapable	sane
uncertain	receptive
unworthy	prayerful
dismayed	

She added that she had now learned the meaning of humility
and meditation. She didn't say that she felt that all her problems
were gone, as is often claimed in other conversion experiences.
Further, there was no self-righteous attitude or rigid, stereotyped,
repetitive, moralistic behavior that is often present in other conversion experiences. She knew she still had many of the problems
of the "before state," but now there was something that was also
"new." The something new felt good, and it gave her hope for a
new life.

As Tiebout sought to understand, he identified two inner
realities that had been changed: one was the sense of omnipotence
and the other was egocentricity. He identified these as infantile
traits that are there at the start of life. As he looked at all the traits
he had seen in the patients with alcoholism, he identified three that
were involved in surrender. He says, "At the start of life the
psyche: (1) assumes its own omnipotence, (2) cannot accept
frustration, (3) functions at a tempo *allegretto* with a good deal of
staccato and *vivace* thrown in" (Tiebout, 1954, p. 612). The third trait
he identified with the descriptive phrase "sense of hurry" or, as

clearly evident in the infant and child, the expectation that there will be immediate satisfaction of needs and desires.

We tend to assume, falsely, that as we grow older we automatically grow up. Instead, the sense of omnipotence and egocentricity of infancy, which Dr. Tiebout refers to as "his majesty the baby," remains deeply embedded, often well-disguised, and functions with a good deal of self-deception. It is possible to be an adult and be emotionally a young child or teenager. No adult ever reaches the full maturity of personhood, emptied totally of omnipotence and egocentricity. According to Dr. Tiebout, even underneath the feelings of inadequacy and inferiority is the infantile omnipotent ego.

There is that within us that tenaciously wants to remain on the throne of our lives, our sense of omnipotence and egocentricity. In our words, attitudes, feelings, and behaviors we can hear the infant inside sometimes shouting, "I want it my way. I want what I want. I want to be in control of all that has to do with my life, and I will prove that I am." We hear that inner reality shouting or saying through the quietness of self-pity, "I want what I want and I want it now." We hear that inner reality loudly and dramatically finding expression in impatience and low frustration tolerance. We hear it in the "why me?" and in the feeling "I am no good," or "I am nobody," or "nobody could love me," or "God could never love and forgive me." The person who makes those last statements has experienced a good deal of hurt and damage, and it will take a lot of caring and helping for the person to see the disguised reality that is really saying, "I am different, unique, and special." It's an inner perception and response that keeps the focus on me and keeps me at the center. It even includes the delusion that I have the power to change the nature of God.

None of us, not even those raised within a healthy home, naturally gets freed up from that inner king. The only way this delusioned reality is altered is by, what my colleague Jim McInerney called, "a sufficient degree of pain." And for some, no degree of emotional or spiritual pain or no amount of blockage seems sufficient to crack the delusion. Some people are born, live, and die with the omnipotent ego fully entrenched and dominating.

Some cannot imagine a life in which the omnipotent ego has surrendered. They see such a life as having no zip or drive or accomplishment or personal payoff. They say it can't work, and it is only an idealized delusion for life in our world. However, Tiebout says, "Life without Ego [in the sense in which it is here presented] is no new conception. Two thousand years ago Christ preached the necessity of losing one's life in order to find it." He also says that Freud could not conceive of life without that Ego (for him the original narcissism of the infant), and therefore Freud was never able to solve this riddle. Freud thought in terms of reducing that Ego, but never of surrender (pp. 612-618).

Tiebout came to the conclusion that when the patient said, "I surrendered," she was saying that something happened to that self-deceiving, infantile, omnipotent inner king entrenched in her being. Whatever happened freed her from its domination, opened up a new way of perceiving life, and provided an opportunity to have some positive attitudes and feelings. Surrender opened the door to emotional and spiritual growth.

Tiebout developed the concept of "compliance versus surrender." Compliance was seen as a purely conscious awareness with an intellectual acceptance, but with the Ego still entrenched on the throne in the unconscious. The self is divided. There is a "yes" but a much more profound and powerful "no." An alcoholic in treatment having come to compliance says, "Nobody has to tell me I am an alcoholic. I've known that for ten years." And during those ten years, he or she has been drinking.

According to Dr. Tiebout, in surrender the conscious and unconscious come together with a fundamental "yes" to the reality of powerlessness. Members of Alcoholics Anonymous are saying much the same thing when they say, "You have admitted it, but have you really accepted it?" It seems clear that a sufficient degree of pain, both emotional and spiritual, is required for surrender. Members have this statement: "Alcohol beats us to our knees." A certain timing is also involved. Surrender is a process, not an event. Moving from denial to compliance to surrender, like all human change, is a process. For some, surrender never comes.

Rev. Carl Anderson, former regional vice-president of Parkside Medical Services Corporation, who for years was involved as a counselor and administrator in alcoholism treatment programs, developed the following categories related to non-surrender and surrender. They indicate the kind of changes that take place in values, commitments, attitudes, feelings and behaviors.

Non-Surrender Dominant	Surrender (Spiritual) Dominant
Value	
Things, money, power, success, sex	People
Goal	
Acquire the above	Quality of relationships
Commitment	
Power, control, do what I want having it my way	Faithfulness, integrity, doing God's will
Achievement	
Competition, getting	Caring for others, giving of self, behaving in ways that enhance self-esteem
Self-worth	
Being superior, being perfect, seeking to avoid vulnerability	Being me, letting others be self, being human, accept limitations, affirm strengths, productivity, responsibility and accountability for attitudes, feelings and behaviors
Internal	
Pride, self-pity, self-preoccupation, insensitivity seeking praise	Trust, humility, gratitude, awareness of others, openness, empathy

One should not infer that spiritual surrender involves the negation (or lack of affirmation) of things, money, power, success, sex, competition or praise. Rather, the inference is that these are not dominating one's life-style with the perception and belief that to have all that is to have life and meaning.

He also developed the following list:

Non-Surrender Dominant	Surrender Dominant
(Conscious-Unconscious)	
No/No or Yes/No	Yes/Yes
Mistrust	Trust
Anxious, tense	Serenity
Hurry, irritability, low frustration tolerance	Let go, Let God
Dishonesty, self-deception	Honesty
Worry about future	Focus on today
Sense of being different, unique	Common identification with others
Anger, resentment, arrogant, deception, pride, belittling self	Forgiving, humble, self-affirmation
Closed	Open to others
Do it yourself, manipulation	Open to help
Superior/inferior	Equal
Keep, selfish, self-seeking	Share, give
Self-pity, pride, lack of humor, take self too seriously	Gratitude, sense of humor about oneself
Excuses/rationalizations	Responsibility, do what I can
Reactive, defensive	Reflective about self from others and own behavior
Doing it all myself	Prayerful
Perfectionism	Growth
My way	Not my will

In spiritual surrender there is an awareness that full surrender is rarely a reality. It can be present in varying degrees or with varying strength. It can be the dominant reality in a person's faith and life-style on a day-by-day basis.

Those in A.A. who do come to such surrender and recovery consistently say that something happened within them that they didn't make happen. They say it happened "by the grace of God." We have also learned that treatment staff can't make this surrender happen, but we have learned that some things can enhance the possibility that surrender will occur. By providing understanding and acceptance of alcoholism as an illness and the alcoholic as a person, and by employer and family confronting the alcoholic with the reality of the alcoholism, the possibility of surrender increases from about 20 percent to about 80 percent. That's a dramatic increase. But it remains clear that humans can't make surrender happen. It is not a conscious decision or action.

Some nonalcoholism clinicians say that surrender sounds magical. It is not magical. It is clinically observable in hundreds of thousands of recovering people. While it is not magical, there is something spiritual in it. Surrender cannot happen without the involvement of the person and the involvement with other people. The alcoholic needs to be involved in relationships that include listening, communicating, learning, and confronting. There needs to be an internal desire or readiness to let go, to quit fighting, and to give in both within the conscious and unconscious, within the intellect and within the guts of the person.

Tiebout writes about the "unstoppable omnipotent" within, which assumes that it never will be stopped, can be stopped, or should be stopped. It remains a potentially dominating and destructive force. When that reality reassumes dominance in the alcoholic, the alcoholic becomes distressed (and usually returns to drinking) in the delusional belief of the omnipotent ego that "I can handle it." Herein lies the value of A.A., where a person learns a new way of life. Included in that way of life is not only the surrender to (and acceptance of) human powerlessness over alcohol, but also learning to live with that reality "one day at a time." At the beginning of each day proper respect needs to be paid to the continuing internal "unstoppable omnipotent." The day is begun by asking for help, and the day is ended with an expression of gratitude.

Many stories could be told about alcoholics who have experienced surrender and have found a new way of life within their pain, brokenness, and human limitation. One day an alcoholic walked into my office without an appointment. He was obviously extremely anxious. He had been sober in A.A. for some months. He desperately wanted to not drink, but he was a nervous wreck. He said that they talked with him about "one day at a time," but there was no way that in his condition he could sustain that regimen. Desperately, he described what his drive home would be like. The four-lane highway he took went by many bars. He would have to ask for help to get past each bar. If today was like the previous days, he would get home and not have taken a drink, but he would be just as miserable as he was now. He knew that wasn't living, and he also knew that he didn't want to drink.

Some six or seven years later he called long distance about getting a friend admitted to treatment. He couldn't believe how well life was going for him. He still had problems, as do other people, but there had been no drinking. He did not recount all the help he had sought within A.A. and outside the organization but he did recall that office visit, his terrible anxiety, and his inability to sustain the "one day at a time." He had to break it down to even smaller segments. Then he said, "If anyone ever would have told me that someday it could be one day at a time in my life—and that I would feel the way I feel now—I would have told them they were crazy."

The Twelve Steps

1. We admitted we were powerless over alcohol—that our lives had become unmanageable.

2. Came to believe that a Power greater than ourselves could restore us to sanity.

3. Made a decision to turn our will and our lives over to the care of God as we understood Him.

4. Made a searching and fearless moral inventory of ourselves.

5. Admitted to God, to ourselves and to another human being the exact nature of our wrongs.

6. Were entirely ready to have God remove all these defects of character.

7. Humbly asked Him to remove our shortcomings.

8. Made a list of all persons we had harmed and became willing to make amends to them all.

9. Made direct amends to such people whenever possible except when to do so would injure them or others.

10. Continued to take personal inventory and when we were wrong, promptly admitted it.

11. Sought through prayer and meditation to improve our conscious contact with God as we understood Him, praying only for knowledge of His will for us and the power to carry that out.

12. Having had a spiritual awakening as a result of these steps, we tried to carry this message to alcoholics, and to practice these principles in all our affairs.

It is important to note that all the steps are written in the past tense. Again there isn't anything magical here. The steps involve action and behavior to bring about change. They have to do with a spiritual way of life. The early group in writing these steps found themselves saying, "This is what we had to do." They were careful not to push their approach on anyone. But they do say to another alcoholic, that if you have an honest desire to become and stay sober, this is what we found we needed to do.

The words "came to believe" in the second step are very important. It indicates that for most of them the second step was a process rather than an event. They recognized that "turning your life over to the care of God" doesn't just happen. There has to be both faith and an active decision. The early group realized that dishonest thinking was inherent in alcoholism, and that recovery and continuing recovery required self-honesty. Somehow—they would say "by the grace of God"—they gained the wisdom to know that the results of their searching fearless moral inventory needed to be admitted in confidence not only to self and to God but also to another human being. The psychiatrist, Paul Tournier, has said, "We become fully conscious only of what we are able to express to someone else" (Keller, 1966, p. 56). Change only comes when you become willing to change. Prayer and meditation were also essential. The early group knew they had hurt others and themselves and that the only way to handle that hurt was by making amends. The most popular books for recovering people in the Alcoholics Anonymous fellowship, besides the big Alcoholics Anonymous book, are the daily meditation books. From their own experience the early group learned that if they didn't share with others what they had received in spiritual blessing—understanding, acceptance, help, hope, and newness of life—they would lose it all again in drinking.

The early group knew that faith and the spiritual way of life didn't come into being in their lives in a vacuum. It came in and through community (in and through their fellowship) in relationship with other human beings. In spirituality there is not only the vertical dimension "God-self" but also the horizontal "self-others" relationship. They had learned a basic spiritual truth: that if we don't meet self and others in our brokenness, pain, and human limitation we never really meet self or others. All of this is not just knowledge—it involves real wisdom.

In spirituality, in alcoholism treatment programs and recovery, there are two prayers that are regularly included through exposure to the Alcoholics Anonymous program. One is called the Serenity Prayer: "God grant me the serenity to accept the things I cannot change, courage to change the things I can change and wisdom to know the difference." This prayer contains the wisdom of understanding and accepting human limitation, human responsibility, and human potential. The prayer with which they end their Alcoholics Anonymous meetings is the Lord's Prayer.

Fred, a recovering alcoholic came into Alcoholics Anonymous with deep resentments toward God, religion, and the church. Fred said to me, "John, have you ever listened to the fellowship pray the Lord's Prayer?" The next time I went to an open meeting (and ever since) I have listened to them pray that prayer. They really pray. The people in this fellowship are keenly aware of what Ernest Kurtz calls their "not-godness." Another phrase of Ernest Kurtz is that an egocentric expectation for life is not only unrealistic and harmful but for alcoholics is literally death. A.A. members have come to believe that in helping each other in their "essential human limitation," there is a power greater than themselves and sufficient for their need and growth.

There are those who for whatever reasons end up their initial recovery experience in this spiritual way of life by becoming fixated. Relationships only exist for them around their alcoholism and in their relationships with other alcoholics in Alcoholics Anonymous. Over time there is no expansion and growth into other relationships. There is no practicing of the principles of the Twelve Steps in all their other affairs. One can speculate as to the various reasons this fixation may occur. Clearly for some there are psychiatric or psychological impairments that were never either adequately identified or effectively treated in the treatment and recovery process. It is important to note this fixation here because it makes clear that there is nothing magical in spirituality, and that although spirituality is believed to be key in treatment and for recovery, a wholistic philosophy is essential in treatment.

How does spirituality, as expressed in the Twelve Steps of Alcoholics Anonymous, get integrated into an overall wholistic philosophy of treatment? Clearly there must be a commitment to this way of life for recovery by those who provide the treatment services. In an interdisciplinary team approach all professional staff members must be knowledgeable of (and comfortable with) spirituality. The professional treatment team should include trained recovering alcoholics who are active in Alcoholics Anonymous.

The program itself should include lectures and discussions on the Twelve Steps. Introduction to Alcoholics Anonymous is presented by members of Alcoholics Anonymous from the community. A.A. meetings are held in the treatment facility and patients are transported to outside meetings. Alumni coordinators are included in the staff to coordinate A.A. volunteer programs. Alcoholics Anonymous volunteers are available to spend time with the patients. Alcoholics Anonymous literature is part of the required reading. The concept of compliance vs. surrender is presented and addressed in the assessment of patients and their progress. Assessment is made of patients' responses to A.A.

In the early days of the program at Willmar State Hospital, patients came voluntarily (although often in response to outside pressure) or were committed for sixty days. Commitment was easy to obtain, and sheriff's officers would drive patients to Willmar. Follow-up studies indicated that those who were committed did just as well as the voluntary admissions. Given the strength of denial and lack of understanding of the disease by the patient, the professional staff learned that it was important to do whatever would be helpful (or necessary) to get people into treatment. Out of this came the development of a program called Intervention. Intervention has proved to be a very effective way of helping people to begin treatment.

However people end up getting into treatment they are somewhere on a continuum from denial, through compliance, to surrender. Where denial is strong (and that occurs quite often) an in-patient program is usually needed because with an out-patient program the drinking would continue. There can be no effective treatment of alcoholism while the person is still drinking. There needs to be special focus with multiple strategies to properly deal with denial or compliance, and to move toward surrender. This is essential for treatment to be effective, because the first step for recovery is surrender.

My belief is that spirituality is a human reality that is clinically observable. There is need for clinical and research psychiatrists and psychologists to give it more attention. Their involvement is essential to help plumb the depths of its meaning and to enlarge our understanding. Spirituality cannot and must not be left to theology alone.

References

Alcoholics anonymous comes of age. (1939). New York: Alcoholics Anonymous World Services, Inc.

Fosdick, H. E. (1939). In *Alcoholics anonymous comes of age.* New York: Alcoholics Anonymous World Services, Inc.

Keller, J. E. (1985). *Let go—Let God.* Minneapolis, Minn.: Augsburg Publishing House.

Keller, J. E. (1966). *Ministering to alcoholics.* Minneapolis, Minn.: Augsburg Publishing House.

Kurtz, E. (1981). *Shame and guilt: Characteristics of the dependency cycle.* Center City, Minn.: Hazelden Educational Materials.

Tiebout, H. (1954). The ego factor in surrender in alcoholism. In *The Tiebout papers.* Center City, Minn.: Hazelden Educational Materials. Reprint from *Quarterly Journal of Studies on Alcohol 15,* 610–621.

Wilson, W. (1939). In *Alcoholics Anonymous comes of age.* New York: Alcoholics Anonymous World Services, Inc.

PART III

EXAMPLES OF EFFECTIVE COLLEGE PROGRAMS

A MODEL COMPREHENSIVE
ALCOHOL PROGRAM
FOR UNIVERSITIES

Jean Kinney

I became involved in the issues of alcohol and the campus by a rather circuitous route, a journey worth recounting. My major professional involvement has been in the area of medical education. One of the challenges to improving the training of medical students is the virtual absence of opportunities for students to work with patients whose problems with alcohol or drugs are just emerging. The bulk of a medical student's training occurs in regional referral hospitals. Thus, the patients that students see are those most likely to have significant medical complications, the result of long drinking careers, for whom the point has long passed when one could provide early intervention.

In considering how to address this dilemma, an obvious solution was to infiltrate the practices of family practice or primary care physicians. This solution was more apparent than real. How many primary care physicians could one expect to offer up their practices for an exploratory, demonstration project? Furthermore, even if we could get a "guinea pig," what would one recommend as the model? The physician's course of action for managing the alcohol dependent person may be fairly clear-cut. But how should the health care system routinely respond to those for whom there is an alcohol problem, but not classic dependence?

At this point, the student health service caught our attention. The college health service seemed to be a primary care setting that would be ideal for exploring and defining a model for delivery of alcohol services. It is a setting that lends itself to early intervention, risk reduction efforts, as well as treatment. As part of the planning

135

process and doing our homework for the pending collaboration with our health service, we consulted the standards/guidelines of the American College Health Association (ACHA), the professional body of college health services (ACHA, 1984).

The ACHA is well known for its progressive stance toward health care issues. Although it no longer formally accredits health services, the Association does promulgate guidelines. These are noteworthy for their scope, incorporating standards for clinical care, record keeping, health promotion, ethics, confidentiality, and the role of the health service as a "public health officer" within the institution. They clearly advocate an aggressive posture in health care maintenance and health care promotion. Indeed, one of the more interesting examples of this is the recommendation that prophylactic administration of rabies vaccine be considered for students doing biological field work; this despite the fact that the Center for Disease Control then indicated an incidence of rabies as 0:100,000 persons. That's aggressive preventative medicine!

Certainly a group that is concerned about rabies would have to be concerned about alcohol/substance abuse. But upon examining the standards, to our disbelief, the ACHA guidelines made absolutely no mention of alcohol or other substances. It occurred to us that some mention of either might be expected to have crept into a fifty-page document, if only by accident, unless such references were specifically purged. In fact that appears to have been the case. Conversations with those involved in drafting the guidelines provided some telling comments. One was that alcohol/substance abuse is not really a health center issue; and that it is being handled, and appropriately so, by deans' offices or other groups on campus. Another comment was that alcohol abuse treatment has not been demonstrated to be effective; therefore it was unfair to burden member schools with delivery of services of undemonstrated value. And finally, alcohol abuse/dependence is generally symptomatic of other more basic issues such as stress or adjustment problems, the "bread and butter" issues of counseling services.

That the ACHA would fail to address alcohol use and

associated problems was mind-boggling. And we're not talking ancient history, or the dark ages of campus programming, but a situation that prevailed in 1985.

This is mentioned not to disparage or castigate the American College Health Association. (It must be noted that living up to its reputation, when this "oversight" was brought to the attention of the ACHA, it took concerted action. The standards that have since been adopted are very thoughtful, comprehensive, and are being combined with efforts to provide staff development to promote their implementation [*Journal of American College Health*, 1987].) Rather it is recounted because it contains almost all of the obstacles to be encountered in efforts to mount campus programs.

Impediments to Campus Programming

What are the major impediments to developing campus programs?

1) *There is a disturbing disregard for scholarly work and research findings.* While certainly not evidencing disinterest, college programmers have demonstrated a notable lack of sophistication in regard to issues of alcohol use and associated problems. This is a source of continuing surprise, possibly because a cherished part of the ethos is that rational discourse, appeal to scholarship, and informed opinion ought to guide behavior.

As a corollary, one finds that idiosyncratic beliefs and personal biases become a substitute for data. That this is as true in institutions of higher education as elsewhere is an irony worth acknowledging. (I have come to see sitting on campus alcohol committees as my year-long Lenten Penance.) By way of example, were there a discussion of the impact of raising the drinking age, the script would be rather predictable:

First Speaker: "I personally was always opposed to the change in drinking age." A shrug of the shoulders, "But we'll have to live with it!"

Second Speaker: "Has the change in the drinking age just succeeded in driving drinking underground? That's something that concerns me."

Committee Chair: "Gee, I don't know, what do those of you in Residential Life see?"

Residential Life Representative: "I sometimes think that is the case; but of course we aren't policemen so I don't really know. I think we need to get the students' views."

All eyes turn to the several student members. They describe their perception of the situation in their own residences. Their observations follow with the statement that their friends concur.

Third Speaker: "Well I continue to be upset by the drinking age issue. It really compounds the difficulty in conducting our campus programs. Plus it deprives us of an opportunity to teach responsible alcohol use."

And by such a process, reality is decreed.

2) As a result, many programs are predicated upon a mix of *misinformation and myth*. For example.

"Heavy drinking is just a stage." This could be termed the developmental hypothesis of spontaneous remission. The implication is that with the acquisition of a diploma, a bit more maturity, and the assumption of adult responsibilities, this developmental phase marked by excessive alcohol consumption will pass. In this formulation no intervention is required. One flaw to this stance is ignoring the reality that alcohol problems can be of such seriousness that the individual may not survive to enjoy a spontaneous remission.

A frequent accompaniment of the above is the belief that alcohol problems in adolescence or young adulthood are, by definition, the result of psychological problems. Accordingly, treatment, were it to be offered, would be geared to dealing with the presumed underlying issues which are being expressed by alcohol abuse. A critically important finding of Vaillant, while prospectively studying adult psychological development, was that those individuals who developed alcohol dependence were indistinguishable from their counterparts who did not, in respect to psychological well-being in earlier life (Vaillant, 1983). Vaillant's research also supported the well-documented finding of the genetic basis for alcoholism, at least among males. Research has typically shown that those with a positive family history are at four times greater risk for developing alcoholism.

"Alcohol problems represent an educational deficit." This is another common stance. In this framework students are seen as uninformed about alcohol or other drugs. Hence, education is seen as a primary intervention. This ignores the fact that our students arrive already having been targets of educational programs in their high schools and communities. Often the education provided is painfully simplistic and amounts to little more than what will fit on a lapel button. And this position also conveniently ignores the fact that changes in knowledge do not necessarily lead to changes in behavior.

Competing with the "informational deficit model" is the approach to alcohol problems as a case of bad manners, essentially a moral issue. Those with alcohol problems are seen as having not only poor attitudes but also questionable values. The challenge of programming becomes to have students "shape up." Discussion of "responsible" drinking can unwittingly reinforce this orientation.

In respect to misconceptions, commonly students are erroneously viewed as non-drinkers thrust into a drinking culture. To the contrary, the majority of students enter college with an established drinking pattern. They not only arrive on campus as drinkers, many qualify as heavy drinkers, defined as having more than five drinks per occasion, a pattern reported by 48 percent of males and 30 percent of females who are high school seniors (Berkelman and Herndon, 1986).

Finally it is widely assumed that students' drinking is "fun." If so, we may be reluctant "to take away" students' pleasures, and/or feel it is puritanical to recommend moderation or elimination of alcohol/drug use. This myth is easily supported if one's own experience with moderate alcohol use is projected on to students with the presumption that the student experience parallels our own, if only in an exaggerated form. For a significant minority drinking isn't fun. There is a price being extracted. Black-outs are frightening. Hangovers are unpleasant. Finding one's roommate has vomited on the floor is disgusting, feels like a violation, and strains a relationship. Waking up, the morning-after, in a virtual stranger's bed feels demeaning, embarrassing, and a violation of values. These are not pleasant experiences. When this reality is not addressed, we invite students to repress and distort their perceptions of their drinking behavior because the reality may be too painful to deal with. Also we allow drugged memories of events to go unchallenged.

3) *The nature of the alcohol field, given its evolution, represents another impediment.* The alcohol field has emerged quite recently as a field of scientific inquiry. Most of the "facts" that many have come to take for granted and assume "have always been known" were only recently established. For example, it was only established in 1953, that abstinence from alcohol, not malnutrition, causes withdrawal and DTs (Victor, & Adams, 1953). In 1967 the AMA first addressed alcoholism as a disease (Proceedings of the House of Delegates, AMA, 1967). In 1968, the Fetal Alcohol Syndrome was first described in the research literature (Lemoine, 1968). In 1971, the genetic basis of alcoholism was established (Goodwin, 1971). Interventions were introduced in 1973 as a means of engaging alcohol de-pendent persons in treatment, rather than believing that they needed to "hit bottom" (Johnson, 1973). It was in 1974 that alcohol *per se*, rather than malnutrition, was documented to be the cause of cirrhosis of the liver (Leiber & DeCarli, 1974). And in 1983 it was established that those who developed alcohol dependence do not have pre-existing psychological problems, thus disproving the theory of an "alcoholic personality" (Vaillant, 1983).

Historically, the modern alcohol treatment field is rooted in the self-help movement of Alcoholics Anonymous (AA) founded in 1935. The initial and virtually exclusive focus of the early alcohol field was upon alcohol dependence and its treat-ment. This was true until the early 1970s when the National In-stitute for Alcohol Abuse and Addictions (NIAAA) was formed, giving impetus to research and training. With the attention being directed to alcohol dependence, as a consequence all alcohol problems were viewed as falling along the spectrum of the progression of the disease of alcoholism. Accordingly all persons with alcohol problems were offered similar treatment—that is, inpatient, and abstinence-oriented. No other options were available. Where treatment was refused, the individual was seen as evidencing denial, or not then being amenable to care. Later, were the individual to develop clear-cut dependence, that provided confirmation of the perception that, if one waits long enough, all alcohol problems ultimately have a single, final common pathway—alcohol dependence.

When the above dependence-oriented model for treating alcohol problems was introduced onto the college campus, it was often met with suspicion. By responding to all clinical problems in an identical fashion, alcohol counselors and professionals became suspect. Often they were viewed not as clinicians, but either as technicians or functioning out of an ideological stance. The myths and misbeliefs that prevailed on the campus in combination with the orientation of the alcohol treatment personnel led to a very strained relationship.

The evolution of campus efforts somewhat parallels the developments in the alcohol treatment field itself. In the early days of campus programming, among those who were most vocal were recovering alumni. Is there a campus alumni magazine that has not published a first person account by a recovering alum? Typically, if not crediting their alma mater with causing their alcohol dependence, these authors point out that the campus proved fertile ground for its later emergence. Implicit in the call for action was a plea for educational efforts to prevent future alcoholism in the present generation of students.

On the campus, the voices of alums were reinforced by those administrators, staff, and faculty concerned with alcohol issues. Not infrequently, among those earliest voices were persons who had personally been touched by alcohol dependence, being either recovering persons or family members.

The earliest campus programs relied almost exclusively

upon educational efforts—such as alcohol days or weeks, out-reach programs to living groups, panels of recovering alumni. These were targeted at the masses in the hopes of reaching that sub-group who in the future might become alcohol dependent. As there was no recognition of other types of alcohol use problems, for the remainder of the student population it was believed that drinking was essentially self-regulating, non-problematic, and hence no intervention was needed.

The Essential Elements of a Campus Program

In approaching what might be the ingredients of a model campus program, it is first necessary to adopt a framework for dealing with the complexity of the problems associated with alcohol use. A framework well suited to the task is the public health model. What is this model and what does this model offer us?

The Public Health Model

The public health model has two major elements: the factors that lead to disease and the interventions needed to promote the total community's health. In considering causes of disease it considers the agent, the host and the environment.

The Agent. Alcohol is widely recognized as a central nervous system depressant. Accordingly, drinking can lead to two different types of problems. There are acute problems that follow on the heels of a single drinking episode, a consequence of drug induced effects. Then there are chronic problems that develop over the longer haul, from the phenomena of tolerance, physical dependence, and the pattern of use. Though for a long time our attention has been upon chronic problems associated with problem use, for young adults, it is the acute problems that may be most significant. It is imperative to distinguish between these two types of problems in developing campus programs.

In respect to alcohol use, it is also important to recognize that alcohol is probably the most potent, self-prescribed pharma-cologic agent. What constitutes a "safe" dose of alcohol or a low risk pattern of use is variable. There is significant variation between individuals as well as for a single individual throughout the life cycle. For example, the incoming freshman with little drinking experience is open to very different problems than is the student who has been a regular and heavy drinker for several years. Similarly, transient circumstances may increase a student's risk for alcohol problems. The use of prescribed medications, or over-the-counter cold preparations, or "recreational" drug use has implications for what constitutes a "safe dose" of alcohol. For some students, medical conditions, such as diabetes, epilepsy, or a mood disorder, can constitute a significant contraindication against more than the most modest alcohol use.

The Host. The risk factors for alcohol dependence have been well documented. The major risk factor for alcohol dependence is a positive family history, compounded by growing up in a culture without clear prescriptions and proscription for drinking. The risk factors for acute problems are less commonly recognized, but are primarily a product of environmental factors.

The Environment. Cultural norms are among the most potent predictors of alcohol problems. The following norms are seen as predictive: (a) solitary drinking; (b) over-permissive norms of drinking; (c) lack of specific drinking norms; (d) tolerance of drunkenness; (e) adverse social behavior tolerated when drinking; (f) utilitarian use of alcohol to reduce tension and anxiety; (g) lack of ritualized and/or ceremonial use of alcohol; (h) alcohol use apart from family and social affiliative functions; (i) alcohol use separated from overall eating patterns; (j) lack of child socializa-tion into drinking patterns; (k) drinking with strangers which increases violence; (l) drinking pursued as a recreation *per se*; (m) drinking concentrated in young males; and (n) a cultural milieu which stresses individualism, self-reliance, and high achievement. In a nutshell, these would seem to be a frighteningly accurate description of college drinking practices (Pattison, 1984).

In addition, the Public Health Model also sets forth the means for maintaining the health of the total community by distinguishing three levels of intervention: those steps to minimize the initial occurrence of illness (primary prevention), the efforts to promote early treatment thereby restoring health (secondary prevention), and providing the necessary follow-up to maintain the health and prevent a recurrence of illness in those who have been treated (tertiary prevention).

Application of the Public Health Framework to College-Age Youth

Though this framework may be elegant and able to incorporate a variety of different phenomena, is alcohol use really a public health issue? Or is it forcing things to adopt this framework? What are the relevant data?

A) A college-age population is essentially a healthy population. (Interestingly, the college health service is possibly the last bastion of primary health care in which acute disease may predominate.) But if a student were to encounter a major health problem resulting in death or disability, the odds are extremely high that alcohol use would be implicated.

B) It may not be widely recognized that the only segment of the population with a declining life expectancy is the age group eighteen to twenty-four years old. Were one to separate out "medical" causes from "social" causes, one finds that it is not "medical conditions" that are attributing to this decline in life expectancy, but "social causes"—accidents, suicide, and homicide. Alcohol figures prominently in each of these categories (Dupont, 1983).

C) A study of lifetime prevalence of major psychiatric disorders indicates that alcohol/substance abuse is the most common psychiatric disorder in the eighteen to forty-five year old age group. It is virtually twice as common as the second most common disorder. This finding is independent of education or social class. So the idea that these individuals are not in the college population is unfounded (Robins and Helzer, 1984)

D) Though increasing, deaths from alcohol and substance use nonetheless remain statistically, relatively infrequent occurrences, although they remain in each of our nightmares. But what is the relationship of alcohol use to those problems that we do encounter daily on our campuses? Trauma and accidents? Unwanted pregnancy? Sexually transmitted disease? Acquaintance rape? What is the relationship of alcohol use and episodes of harassment of minority students, women, or gay students? How does alcohol use fit into vandalism and academic failure? Though the data may remain sparse, the hypothesis that alcohol use is a factor in each of these is not unreasonable. Interestingly, institutions that have gathered descriptive data on some of these problems have been reluctant to publish the findings for fear of the bad press, alumni concern, effect on the applicant pool, or other consequences to the community.

Beyond the case that can be made for alcohol use as a genuine public health problem, the framework proves functional in other ways. It fosters an integrated approach. It recognizes the need for multiple types of intervention and gets away from the tendency to look for the "magic bullet"—the single cure that will completely eliminate the problem. The model also can provide us our greatest leverage for intervention, while providing a rationale and imperative to act. Simultaneously, framing the problems of alcohol use as a public health issue can reduce opposition. It is hard to be against health. On the other hand, the campus community can be polarized by other approaches.

Features of a Comprehensive Program

The Rutgers University's Committee on the Use of Alcohol, in its report to the university made the following observation: "Alcohol use is a complicted topic. Our Committee spent a good deal of time struggling to find a way to think about alcohol. Once we agreed on how to think about alcohol use, our work was simplified" (Rutgers University Committee on the Use of Alcohol, 1981). That document was one of the earliest efforts to articulate a comprehensive campus program. It remains commendable for its scope, the process it sets forth, and the recognition that it is essential to establish both prescriptions and proscriptions for behavior. It represents the standard that we might all use for dealing with this topic.

In designing a comprehensive program, all sectors of the community need to be included. The following (Rutgers University Committee on the Use of Alcohol, 1981; Kinney, & Peltier, 1986; Task Force on Alcohol and Drugs, 1987) are examples of the type of efforts that might be included in a comprehensive campus program:

Health Service Activities
- Broad Community Health Education.
- Public Health Officer
  Bring drinking practices that are potentially harmful to the attention of appropriate groups.
  Develop emergency procedures for the institution, with guidelines for handling intoxicated persons, definitions of medical emergencies clearly noted.
  Consultation
- Alcohol History as part of Initial Health Record
- Format of Medical Records
  Methods must be instituted to allow identification of an emergent alcohol use problem, something that is difficult when medical records are organized solely around clinical encounters.
- Individualized Patient Education
  Assure that every student receives individual patient education related to his or her own alcohol use, discussion of Blood Alcohol Content, drinking patterns, and any absolute or relative contraindications for alcohol use.
- Outreach Programs for Students at Risk
- Clinical Services
  Implement routine screening, evaluation, interventions, referral for treatment, monitoring of students with acute problems, monitoring persons in treatment, or those who have been treated to avoid relapse.
  A.A. group for students
  Develop protocols that specify clinical encounters warranting routine alcohol evaluation

Residential Life Activities
- Norms for Living Groups
  In an effort to articulate normative behavior, have students in living units define what drinking-related behavior is regarded as unacceptable and offensive.
- Risk Management Groups
  Establish "risk management groups," to review any alcohol-related incident, to review alternative actions that might have been taken, and to discuss actions to reduce future risk.
- Protocols for Emergency Situations, inform students of the procedures
- Alternative social activities
- Protocols for residence hall advisors
  These should clearly define steps to be taken if concern arises about a student.
- Consultation for Resident Hall Advisors
  Efforts to support Residence Advisors, and mechanisms to respond to their questions is key to implementing any protocols.
- Living spaces designated for non-drinkers

Greek Organizations
- Consultation on Drinking Practices
  The "fire marshall" approach to help review potential dangerous or problemmatic practices and discuss ways of eliminating these is helpful.
- Elimination of "required" drinking (i.e., drinking games)
- Guidelines for serving of alcoholic beverages (i.e., labeling of alcohol content of "pre-mixed" beverages, hours beverages are served, training of bartenders)
- Non-drinking monitors at social events
- Educational Programs
- Training of Social Chairs

Tasks for the Administration
- Develop a comprehensive alcohol policy
- Develop programs for impaired faculty

- Support for the campus alcohol programs should be adequate
- Mandated clinical evaluations
  Students with a suspected alcohol problem, an alcohol-related disciplinary offense, or in cases of academic failure should be evaluated for a potential alcohol problems.
- Insurance Coverage
  Students, faculty, and staff should be assured of adequate coverage for alcohol/substance use treatment.

Aids to Faculty
- Education on alcohol and academic performance
- Protocols for action for a suspected alcohol problem
- Alcohol issues in intellectual life of community
  Alcohol-related issues are well suited as a vehicle for illustration of course material (public policy, history of social movements, women's studies, and the role of the liquor industry in the suffrage movement, biochemistry, etc.)
- Information services to facilitate alcohol lecture preparation
- Foster research efforts on alcohol-related topics
- Impaired Faculty Program
  An Impaired Professors Program should also be able to deal with issues beyond alcohol/substance use (e.g., Alzheimers Disease, mood disorders)
- Consultation on concerns involving family
  Seeking help for alcohol or substance use problems can often entail a sequence of steps, a series of successive approximations of seeking help.

Tasks for Athletic Programs
- Workshops/retreats for coaches and trainers
  These are directed toward beginning to define standards that the athletic department will actively promote and enforce.
- Leadership training for team captains
  This provides the basis for captains working with their teams to promote norms of use and non-use for the team as preparation for implementing alcohol/substance abuse programs.
- Team educational programs
  These should cover the specifics related to alcohol and

performance and also other substance use including "performance enhancing" drugs.

- Teams setting standards of use

  This entails discussion and identifying use that is acceptable to the team, that which is not, and specifying ways in which the team, as a group, will enforce its collective decisions.

- Health education and fitness programs.

  Whether for the community or students only, these should incorporate some alcohol use information.

- Policies on alcoholic beverages at sporting events

Services for Alumni

- Information and education about the efforts on campus

- Alcohol use in alumni gatherings

  Steps need to be taken to promote use of alcohol at alumni social functions that is consistent with the norms being promoted on campus.

- Recovering alcoholics

  Alumni gatherings ought to provide for meeting places for recovering alcoholics and information be provided on area A.A. meetings

- Academic offerings in "alumni colleges"

The Role of Other Groups

- Campus Police

  Establish and train in emergency procedures

- Campus Chaplaincy

  Address issues of alcohol use as a pastoral concern with individuals and the impact in the spiritual life of the community.

- Student Supportive Services

  Groups such as study skills centers ought to be alert to alcohol use problems and be able to make referrals for evaluation, plus be a source of public information on the impact of alcohol use on academic performance.

- Employee Assistance Packages for Student Employees

Each of the above elements can also be viewed with respect

to different levels of prevention. A program effort (such as de-signating sections of a dormitory for those who are non-drinkers) may be both primary prevention for acute problems and at the same time serve as tertiary prevention for a recovering student.

Establishing a Program: Process, the Neglected Element

If the above are potential components of a comprehensive program, how does one go about putting such a program in place?

The Institutional Agenda

The first requirement is to establish an institutional com-mitment to addressing alcohol and substance use in a real way, to make this a central item on the institution's agenda. To accomplish this requires more than a one-hour meeting of senior adminis-trators, or polling faculty, or a brief cursory presentation to trustees. It requires grappling with the issue sufficiently so that not to act becomes impossible. It requires sufficient consideration to recog-nize the dimensions of the problems and a realistic appreciation of what will be required to address them. This might be facilitated by the preparation of a "White Paper" or some similar effort as a vehicle for the institution's consideration.

Planning

With the institution having decided to address alcohol and substance use issues, the next step is not to run out and hire a coordinator, or alcohol resource person, delegate the alcohol issue to him or her, allowing everyone else to go about their business as usual.

If one wishes to begin to make a dent in community norms, drinking practices, and attitudes, this is not something that is readily achieved or accomplished by decree. Consider for a moment the kind of planning that goes into a presidential search, or is the prelude to a major and multi-year fund-raising effort, or is entailed in making curriculum revision. Outside consultants are called in, other institutions are contacted, a plan for action is sketched out. That kind of approach is required. For a change of the magnitude desired, strategic planning for a multi-year time-frame is necessary. Bear in mind that while the last bastions of tradition, paradoxically, institutions of higher education also have the capacity to remake themselves over a very brief period. In a four-year period, the student body turns over. Very quickly the institutional memory can be reshaped and new patterns defined as "that's how we always have done it."

To make a concerted effort will also require an infusion of fiscal resources. The alternative is to spend more over an extended period and make relatively few inroads.

The effective campus program will also require sophisticated leadership, in addition to line staff. In terms of personnel, consider the common advertisement for someone to direct campus alcohol programs: "Individual with experience in alcohol education in college setting, clinical skills, experience in program planning, . . . salary competitive." We look for the Renaissance man or woman and offer $28,500! Instead, consider what a colleague refers to as the "NFL-recruiting-principle: go for the best athlete and worry about position later." Beyond being knowledgeable about alcohol, which is relatively easily acquired, if one knows one is not informed, additional expertise is needed. Analytic skills and community development skills are a big plus. Knowledge about adolescent development certainly is helpful. How does one factor alcohol use into the developmental process? What functions is the current alcohol use pattern serving? The writing on this topic in the alcohol literature is fairly narrow, focusing upon adolescents' experimentation with alcohol, or sense of being invulnerable, or the risk taking that is characteristic at this age. But this certainly isn't the whole picture. How does alcohol use fit into developmental tasks? It appears to relate to experimentation not with alcohol, but with intimacy, or means of trying on roles, without needing to assume responsibility for the outcome, and other larger issues.

An important early step in planning and implementing a program is collecting basic descriptive data about actual alcohol use patterns on one's own campus. Without some sense of the distribution of drinking practices among students, we may unwittingly adopt a distorted perception of campus alcohol use. By way of comparison, consider alcohol use patterns in the general population. Among adults over the age of twenty-one, 30 percent of the population are essentially non-drinkers, consuming less than one drink per year. Of the remainder of the adult population, there is the 50 percent who drink, but as a group consume only 20 percent of all the alcohol. So that leaves only a fifth of the population (pun not intended), or 20 percent consuming 80 percent of all alcoholic beverages. Even among that group of heavy drinkers, one finds that 50 percent of all alcohol is consumed by 7 percent of the population (National Institute on Alcohol Abuse and Alcoholism, 1980). An important implication of these consumption patterns is that, as a nation, we could cut alcohol consumption by one half and only "inconvenience" a small segment (7%) of the population.

What does one find on the college campus? Presumably there will be fewer abstainers than in the general population, but similarly there appears to be a heavy-drinking sub-group. A survey of alcohol use at Dartmouth College revealed the following findings:

Pattern of Collegiate Alcohol Consumption in a "Typical" Week

Number drinks "typical" week	% of total ETOH consumed	Cumulative % ETOH consumed	Cumulative % of population
0.0	0	0	9.6
0.0–1	1.5	1.5	24.6
1.5–2	1.3	2.8	30.5
2.5–5	10	13	50.3
6.0–10	23	36	74.1
11.0–15	18	54	85.3
16.0–20	15	69	92.1
22.0–30	17	86	97.4
40.0–50	14	100	100.0

N = 343

Information on the spectrum of drinking practices is also very useful in the clinical realm. It provides a context that allows recognition of those who are the heavy drinkers by the campus' norms. Tending not to be aware of the number of light drinking students, it is very easy to accept a student's assertion that "everyone drinks like I do."

An important component of an institutional effort is an alcohol policy. To my mind an alcohol policy should not read like a penal code. Rather I would suggest a clear, crisp statement of the institution's stance toward alcohol use and the steps and means it intends to use in addressing these. I would consider an alcohol policy to be analogous to statements about academic honesty. In such statements, the institution's position is clear. The standards set for members' behavior are unambiguous. There is not, however, an effort to establish comprehensive policing efforts to assure compliance. However, if violations of the honor code come to attention, without hesitation they will be treated as serious breaches of the ethos underpinning the community's intellectual life.

Beyond the red herring of "Can we enforce an alcohol policy?" and opting to go no further than creating "all-the-policy-we-think-we-can-enforce," there is often an accompanying concern with liability. While one need not be foolish, the reality is that no institution can perfectly protect itself from suit in our litigious society. The institution is the deep pocket. The best protection may well be the steps that are being recommended.

Implementation

A comprehensive program needs to involve all sectors of the community. This does not mean that everyone need be a "true believer" in the same fashion. For some, public relations may be a major concern; for others it may be institutional liability; for still others it may be the record on the playing field or not jeopardizing the school's status with the NCAA by coming up with positive urine screens. For others the quality of life will be a major motivator, and for others the academic life. For some, it will be a health concern or it may be personal identification with the issues of children of alcoholics or alcohol dependence. A model program can encompass (and must encompass) all these motives, not deeming some as more legitimate and noble than others. Ultimately campus-wide involvement occurs when alcohol issues are recognized as intruding upon each of us.

The lessons learned in working with medical school faculty around curriculum change seem relevant to other types of institutional change. The basis for engaging the faculty and the institution was as collaborators in an experiment. Three questions were set forth at the beginning of the project as questions to be addressed: "Is there a constructive way to teach young physicians what is currently known about alcohol and the care of the alcoholic?" "Why is that knowledge so difficult to integrate into the medical school curriculum?" and finally, "Why are students and faculty so often seemingly disinterested in what is clearly one of the nation's most complex public health problems?" In this framework, the atmosphere was set to permit, if you will, freedom to "muddle through." It invited us to consider process and examine efforts as candidly as possible. In this approach we avoided the all too common practice of labeling people as deficient, remiss, or evidencing poor attitudes by not having been previously involved with the topic of alcohol. It was not a campaign to have people shape up.

In defining the need for change, the one segment of the community often ignored is the students. Too often what happens is that others formulate policy and make the basic decisions, and put it to the students for some review and comment. And then the policy formulators get bogged down spending much time agonizing over how to engineer students' acceptance. For example, on our own campus during freshman orientation, there is a concerted effort to address alcohol issues. There are a number of different and innovative programs. However, why can't we also be completely frank with them. Why not say:

> Look, there is a serious problem in this institution
> as in society with alcohol use. It does not admit to

easy solutions. We need to call upon you to become involved with us in grappling with this
issue. None of us has a corner on truth, we will
have some trial and error in the process. We must
work together, because none of us has the luxury of
doing nothing.

Education is a common element of programs. But one's
expectations for broad-based community education programs
should not be too high. Their greatest significance may be their
impact upon the general climate, and in that fashion facilitating
other program initiatives. Education is more than the provision
of facts. The more effective approaches are those that allow information to be processed and reflected upon, and those targeted
to meet special needs. Providing education in large measure is
recognizing educational opportunites. For example, a student
has been in treatment, returns to campus and discovers his fraternity brothers and friends seem to be uncomfortable about the
implications for their relationships with him. Such situations,
properly engineered provide an opportunity to sit down with
students, around a specific situation that involves them, to discuss dependence, treatment, and the role of friends in providing
support for sobriety, and openly discussing the do's and don't's.

A basic issue that every campus with an alcohol program
will need to confront is "What will be our threshold of concern
in respect to individuals?" Or to put that another way, what is
the institution prepared to overlook. I would like to suggest
that the threshold of concern be very low. Whether an alcohol
incident represents an isolated event or a chronic problem will
not be outwardly and immediately apparent. This is the place to
keep clearly in mind that the consequences of acute problems
can be as disastrous as those connected with alcohol dependence.

The clinical model that is worth considering is that all untoward incidents involving alcohol use must be taken seriously
and warrant evaluation/assessment. Take as a guide those steps
which would be appropriate were you faced with any other
suspected serious medical condition. When something atypical is

suspected, generally a referral follows for further assessment or a diagnostic workup. If the suspected problem is not confirmed, the person initiating the referral does not have to be apologetic! The accepted stance is always to err on the conservative side.

Here too, a chronic disease perspective is exceedingly useful. With any chronic disease the most significant actions are those taken prior to the clear onset of the full-blown disease process. An example may be illustrative—heart disease. A young male comes into his doctor's office. He is overweight, both smokes and drinks, consumes a cholesterol-laden diet, never exercises, and has a family history of males who keel over prior to age fifty of coronary disease. From his internist's perspective, he is a walking time-bomb. The physician does not have to be convinced that this individual will be true to his genes to be comfortable intervening. It is sufficient to know that statistically this individual is at risk. Even if wholly asymptomatic, the physician will feel perfectly comfortable urging rather drastic changes in life style to reduce risk. (These changes for our hypothetical young man are equivalent to the changes associated with abstinence or, for a college student, the drastic alteration of drinking behavior.) If the physician in question were really on top of it, he would refer this patient to several groups, load him down with pamphlets, and through continuing contacts monitor compliance and provide encouragement and support. This model assures the optimal management of problems associated with alcohol use or dependence. From a management point of view, the most relevant question is no longer, "Is this person alcoholic, or an alcohol abuser, or just naive and unlucky?" The central question becomes, "If this person continues drinking, as they have, is he or she at risk for a serious alcohol incident or developing alcohol dependence?"

In this example, we need recognize that interventions with individuals can be potently reinforced by the community, or be wholly neutralized. For our hypothetical young man, the chances of his making significant changes will be improved when he is bombarded by thirty-second TV spots on the dangers of hypertension, or when he goes to a restaurant and finds entrees identified as low cholesterol, low sodium. Or when his employer encourages exercise by providing lockers and showers for the noon-time joggers.

Alcohol Incidents

These refer to drinking which results in negative consequences for the student. Typically these incidents would not have occurred were alcohol not in the picture. It's important not to make any presumptions (i.e., that the incident has been sufficient to teach the student a lesson and guarantee that there will be no further difficulties). Don't presume that the embarrassment, guilt, discomfort, or anxiety was sufficient to alter future behavior. It is vitally important that the incident not be treated as a joke by peers. All those who may have contact with the student—be it emergency room personnel, or deans, or campus police, or peers—all need to acknowledge the role of alcohol in what occurred. The actual or potential seriousness needs to be made clear. In part, what allows a chronic alcohol problem to blossom is the absence of feedback by others in the face of alcohol-related incidents.

Following an alcohol incident, education and risk reduction efforts are central. The goal is to lower the likelihood of the student's getting into trouble in the future. We can't presume that students, however bright and sophisticated, are sufficiently knowledgeable about alcohol and its actions to figure out what the risks are. Education underpins any risk-reduction efforts. This should be detailed and tied to what has transpired. The underlying message is that if a student is going to use the drug alcohol he or she needs to be fully informed about it. Along with education, an inventory of drinking practices is called for: reviewing the settings in which drinking takes place; the activities that accompany drinking; a family history of alcoholism or medical conditions which may be adversely influenced by alcohol use. For any drinking practices likely to place the student at increased risk, specific behavioral prescriptions can be developed. For example, what might a person do when faced with being a passenger in a car with an intoxicated driver? Identify potential problems and help the student think through—ahead of time—what should be done.

When such risk-reduction efforts occur, were future alcohol problems to arise, it can be assumed that the student is not ignorant, but that a more chronic problem is emerging.

Alcohol Abuse

Alcohol abuse is a pattern of high risk alcohol use. From a physiological standpoint, as physical dependence and loss of control have not been established, then moderation of drinking practices is possible. However, for the college student this can nonetheless represent a monumental feat. Consider the student active in a fraternity, which has an open tap twenty-four hours a day, and at least three evenings per week when drinking is common among the brothers. To change drinking patterns will require marked changes in how the student organizes his life, who his friends are, and what activities constitute recreation. To achieve change of such magnitude will require the student be engaged in more than a Dutch uncle talk!

Students diagnosed as having alcohol abuse cannot be expected—nor expect themselves—to alter their alcohol use so dramatically on their own. Formal treatment for alcohol abuse is indicated. Techniques originally used with alcohol-dependent persons to teach controlled drinking are likely to be very useful here. Given the bad press that controlled drinking treatment approaches have had, I prefer the phrase "moderation of alcohol use" as the goal of treatment. Monitoring efforts to moderate alcohol use is imperative. Through this process, over time, evidence may mount that there is loss of control over alcohol use or a preoccupation with drinking, or that alcohol use has assumed an almost organizing role in the student's life. If that be the case, abstinence and traditional alcoholism treatment is needed. Practically speaking, the differential diagnosis of alcohol dependence will be made if efforts to address alcohol abuse prove unsuccessful.

Clinically the dilemma of distinguishing alcohol abuse from alcohol dependence is more apparent than real. Here again the framework of chronic disease is useful. Either diagnostic category requires a modification of drinking practices. The differential diagnosis can be made over time. A student's ability or inability to change drinking practices will be telling. A significant factor in this may be the attitudes and perceptions of peers, and their appreciation of the potential dangers and their ability to provide support for less risky alcohol use.

Final Comments

Something that may strike others as a bit unimportant (but I consider very important) is the language that we use in discussing alcohol use and alcohol problems. Language in a very subtle but powerful manner molds our thinking. The alcohol field as a whole uses language that originated in the treatment sphere. Much has very moralistic overtones that I believe is very functional in the treatment realm. But, to my mind, it is dysfunctional in education, prevention, and efforts for early identification. For example, alcoholics are described as "con artists," as "manipulative" or as "denying," which often is a synonym for lying. These do not sound like symptoms of an illness but character traits. If we want to use a health model we need to adopt language that is consistent with, and promotes that perspective. Part of this is avoiding judgmental, moralistic terms. For example, the title of this volume speaks of alcohol use and misuse. "Misuse" to me connotes finger-wagging, the clear implication being misbehavior and being "bad." If those for whom we have concerns do not consider those terms to be accurate, fair descriptors, then we create a significant barrier that can be avoided. Why use charged language when there is more neutral language available?

I don't know how apparent my own efforts have been to avoid some phrases and to use alternatives. Alcohol dependence has become the preferred term for alcoholism. Beyond using this to reflect current professional usage, reflect upon the implications of using alcoholic as a noun. The individual is reduced to nothing more than his or her disease. Unless we are clergy and/or trying to address the ethical and moral dimensions of alcohol use, to speak about "responsible" drinking is unfortunate. Are those with "high risk alcohol use patterns" by definition irresponsible? Admittedly the phrase is more cumbersome, but it has the advantage of more accurately conveying what I think we want to address.

Another observation that may be trite but needs to be said is that in our efforts, we must remain vigilant that we not abandon common sense. There is the temptation at times to "finally take a stand"—which usually occurs after a lengthy period of vacillating, wishy-washy behavior—when we decide to do something dramatic, a something that often is not well thought out. An incident that comes to mind is one that involved our local high school. Several years ago, there was a growing concern about student drinking. There were the usual concerns—unchaperoned parties with drinking, parents allowing alcohol to be served in their homes, drinking and driving, bringing alcohol to school dances or coming to dances after drinking. That year the soccer team had had an outstanding season and in the play-offs had made it to the game for the state championship. A parent put a bottle of champagne on the bus. The team won. In the course of the hooping and hollering, someone remembered the champagne. The players proceeded to pop the cork, showering one another with the contents. Then came the uproar. In the aftermath, the team members refused to tell who got it from the bus. Interestingly, the parent involved never "fessed up" either. The outcome was the following: the next year's team would not be allowed to participate in any post-season games, regardless of their playing record. Beyond all the questions of delaying punishment for that period, or penalizing players who may not have been present, there's the ultimate irony. Not only were they following the well-established tradition we witness at the conclusion of every professional championship game, it may have been the most appropriate, nondestructive use of alcohol ever displayed in the school. But alas, this was the time to "put the foot down." While possibly an overly dramatic example, nonetheless, by acting in fits and starts, we can undermine much of our efforts.

In conclusion, consider how one will know if the efforts have been successful. There are a number of parameters that can be used as measures of program impact. These might in clude levels of dorm damage, numbers of emergency visits to the local hospital emergency room, the number of cases that come before the campus judiciary system involving alcohol, and so forth.

However, there is another whole dimension, that does not as easily lend itself to measurement. But in this arena, too, we can judge what has taken place. A colleague related the following story, one that he happened to hear only by chance.

A fraternity member at the prodding of concerned friends was seen by a counselor and eventually entered residential care. This set off a wave of referrals in the house. One turned out to be the President, who was treated as an outpatient and became active in A.A. Following Rush, the first house meeting with the new pledge class was held. Each person in turn introduced himself. One of the first persons, in a take-off of A.A., added "And I'm an alcoholic." This was met with by tittering and laughter; and each subsequent person introduced himself in a similar fashion, concluding with "and I'm an alcoholic." Then it was the President's turn. He was reported to have looked around at each person, and introduced himself in a quiet but forthright way—"I'm Joe, and I really am an alcoholic." Dead silence.

Ultimately, the goal is for change to permeate throughout the community, so that everyday encounters between persons, of the sort that go unnoticed by others, will embody increased awareness, and an appreciation of the problems that can accompany alcohol use. A moment as described lasting all of ten seconds embodies many year's work and becomes the most eloquent testimony to our efforts.

Acknowledgment

Reprinted by permission of the publisher from *Clinical manual of substance abuse* (St. Louis: Mosby-Year Book, 1991), pp. 258–269.

References

American College Health Association. (1984). Recommended standards and practices for a college health program, Fourth Edition (1984). *Journal of American College Health, 32,* whole issue.

Berkelman, R. L., & Herndon (1986). Patterns of Alcohol Consumption and Alcohol-Related Morbidity and Mortality. *Morbidity and Mortality Weekly Report, 35,* 1–5.

Dupont, R. L. (1983). Teenage drug use: Opportunities for the pediatrician. *Journal of Pediatrics, 102,* 1003–1007.

Goodwin, D. W. (1971). Is alcoholism hereditary? *Archives of General Psychiatry, 25,* 545–548.

Johnson, V. (1973). *I'll quit tomorrow.* New York: Harper and Row.

Journal of American College Health. (1987). Students, alcohol, and college health: A special issue, *36.*

Kinney, J., Peltier, D. (1986). A model alcohol program for the college health service. *Journal of American College Health, 34,* 229–233.

Leiber, C. S., & DeCarli, L. M. (1974). An experimental model of alcohol feeding and liver injury in the baboon. *Journal of Medical Primatology, 3,* 153–163.

Lemoine, P., Harousseau, H. et al. (1968). Les enfants de parents alcooliques: Anomalies observees. *Ouest Medical, 21,* 476–482.

Pattison, E. M. (1984). Cultural level interventions in the arena of alcoholism. *Alcoholism: Clinical and Experimental Research, 8,* 160–164.

Proceedings of the House of Delegates, 20th Clinical Convention, Nov. 28–30, 1966. Las Vegas: *American Medical Association,* 1967.

Robins, L. N., & Helzer, J. E. (1984). Lifetime prevalence of specific psychiatric disorders in three sites. *Archives of General Psychiatry, 41,* 949–958.

Rutgers University Committee on the Use of Alcohol, William David Burns, Chair. 1981.

Task Force on Alcohol and Drugs. (1987). Standards on alcohol and substance use, misuse, and dependency. *Journal of American College Health, 36*, 60–63.

National Institute on Alcohol Abuse and Alcoholism. (1980). The public health approach to problems associated with alcohol consumption: A briefing. Publication No. (ADM) 8980–994.

Vaillant, G. (1983). *Natural history of alcoholism.* Cambridge, Mass.: Harvard University Press.

Victor, M., & Adams, R. D. (1953). The effect of alcohol on the nervous system. *Association for Research Nervous and Mental Disease 32,* 526–673.

College Programming : The Full Sweep

Bruce E. Donovan

Colleges do little to regulate the use of alcohol. Policies are written into the undergraduate rules mainly to protect the institution in case a student dies or is injured. They provide the institution with an excuse for disciplinary action. Positive programs to prevent the abuse of alcoholic beverages are skimpy and ineffective. Off-campus fraternities get little or no supervision until trouble occurs. This may begin to change with more restrictive laws and an enormous increase in lawsuits. Till then don't expect your college to protect you from your own worst instincts. You are responsible for your drinking habits and no one else. (Clark, p. 214)

This recent commentary is especially distressing since it is offered to potential applicants by a *quondam* college president: it is a seasoned, inside view. Nor is it a unique commentary: Ernest Boyer reports bleak views, more diplomatically phrased, from other college administrators (Boyer, 1987). Perhaps most discouraging is that Straus and Bacon (1953), while writing from a different perspective and optimistic about the good that colleges might do, sounded a very similar tone in *Drinking in College* fully forty years ago.

Happily, not every campus is quite so mired in self-interest and benign neglect. True, changes in the legal drinking age and a fear of litigation may be the most common goads to action, and initiative may, therefore, be sluggish. Nonetheless, societal concern with general health issues and drug use in particular

165

provide happier omens than in the past. Institutions of higher learning may be coming to understand that drug programming is not only a hedge against legal difficulties, but also a good way to assure realization of their most basic goals. The promise of progress may be brighter now than ever.

Background

Drinking in College (Straus & Bacon, 1953) is usually cited as the first major volume on alcohol on campus. Ironically, the authors cautioned against regarding collegiate drinking as a thing too removed from drinking in society at large. "When we were considering the title for this book the choice rapidly narrowed to two: *College Drinking* and *Drinking in College*. It was suggested that the former was preferable because it was shorter, and because in any event this may very well be referred to as 'that book about college drinking.' But *College Drinking* was rejected because there is no evidence that such a pheno-menon exists" (Straus & Boyer, 1953). Nonetheless, the college context has become a distinct topic of concern.

The yield of specialized bibliography for the 1950s and 1960s is sparse, but from that point increasingly to the present, theoretical and applied publications on collegiate subjects have multiplied steadily. A review of the current literature, how-ever, still yields an uneven harvest. Academic initiatives and the involvement of faculty are almost untouched. Information on policy development is scarce. Work on special populations— for women, minorities, gays and lesbians, older students, and until quite recently even athletes—is also very limited. On the other hand, considerable research is available on demographics, peer counseling, and counseling in general; and most recently information on college health has been especially helpful (*Journal of American College Health*, 1987). One also hopes for new initiatives from the range of projects currently funded by the Department of Education through the Fund for the Improve-ment of Post-Secondary Education (FIPSE).

Staffing of individual college programs has also impeded progress. Too frequently responsibility is shouldered by one whose major interest and training has not been in the area of alcohol or other drug concerns. "When present, these [treatment and intervention] appear to be a reflection of the training and personal experience of the individual responsible for alcohol efforts rather than a statement of institutional policy" (Kinney & Peltier, 1986, p. 229). With success of treatment and intervention programs, and those in prevention as well, dependent on the initiative of one individual, and with programs stalled when personnel change, progress cannot but be erratic.

Several initiatives from the last decade or so are noteworthy. The federally sponsored 50 Plus 12 Project, which in the mid-1970s convened representatives from one university in each of the fifty states and twelve individuals from private or minority schools, was designed to procure information on campus drinking, on existing programs which addressed the issue, and on current needs; to disseminate information on alcohol; and to encourage new programming. In describing this project, Kraft (1976) provides yet further evidence for the abiding administrative resistance to engagement with alcohol issues. Denial of the need for action, largely based on a sense that unless alcoholics were to appear in troubling numbers, nothing needed to be done; despair, contrarily, at the scope of the problem, and the inhibiting effect of such problems among faculty and staff; frustration that alcohol information programs did not curb unruly behavior; and an eager, straightforward simplicity in thinking a dry campus the best solution characterized administrative positions.

The National Institute on Alcohol Abuse and Alcoholism supported this endeavor and funded two other special additional initiatives. The University of Massachusetts in Amherst housed the University Alcohol Education Project, primarily focused on undergraduates (Kraft, 1984), and the University of Missouri-Columbia received funds to develop campus employee assistance programming, and to stimulate similar development on other campuses through technical support and annual conferences.

Brown University, without federal support, in 1977 appointed an Associate Dean for Chemical Dependency. This dean, in distinction from figures responsible for chemical dependency on other campuses, was a member of the academic administration and responsibile for initiatives that would fuse concern for undergraduate and graduate students with attention to faculty and staff. The goal was to locate programs firmly in the context of the University's central purposes.

Although activity at Massachusetts and Missouri provided certain paradigms, few models existed for the synthetic program that Brown envisioned (Donovan, 1981; Goodale, 1978). For alcohol issues one could look to the model of BACCHUS, student-focused and social in its concern. But the model of a comprehensive program for all constituencies was not at hand. In any event, adaptation would become an operating principle because Brown, like every other campus, has its own ethos that must not be violated in program development. A strong concept of community, together with the practical matters of size and limited resources, suggested common programs open to all campus populations, as well as discrete initiatives for particular constituencies. Such a campus-wide effort is still not common, even though the utility of a broad approach has been seen for some time. For example, in 1980 it was observed:

> . . . the natural environment in which students function plays a vital role in the level of knowledge, degree of responsibility in attitudes and incidence of negative consequences related to alcohol use. Therefore, educators concerned about the prevention of alcohol abuse should seek to create comprehensive campus-wide approaches to alcohol education. Such approaches should be designed to impact on individual student attitudes as well as create environments which encourage students to practice the responsible behaviors being promoted. (Gonzalez, 1980, p. 11)

The contrast was striking between Brown's initiatives and the more amply funded programs at the two larger state universities. The avowed concern with faculty, staff, and students; a determination to deal to the extent feasible with all three groups together; and a common focus on prevention, education and treatment most distinguished Brown's efforts.

Progress was not always smooth, nor appropriately informed, nor is the job in any sense "done." But the Brown campus continues to be a place where resources are available for all constituencies and where issues of substance abuse are openly discussed.

Clearly this has been a genuine community effort: no one individual could effect the changes now in place. The governing principle has been and is to encourage others, whatever their positions, to assume appropriate responsibility for part of an issue for which many are in part accountable: security, deans of students, counselors, student activities personnel, catering services, athletics, university relations, health services and so on.

The current *modus operandi* is monthly meetings for the approximately fifteen administrators charged with day-to-day responsibility for some aspect of drug issue. The group includes those who make policy and those whose jobs are its implementation. Smaller configurations of the membership consider particular topics (e.g., enforcement, freshman orientation, and disposition of complex student cases). The large meetings afford conversation among administrators who have quite different perspectives and different responsibilities—e.g., legal, medical, social, academic—and allow everyone to observe the biases (professional and personal) which inform the work of colleagues and to debate points of difference as policy and procedures are developed.

Policy

A study of national surveys taken in 1979, 1982, and 1985 claims that "responsible standards and activities for addressing alcohol use and abuse are increasing on college and university campuses" (Anderson & Gadaleto, 1986, p. 499). This conclusion is surely open to interpretation. We recall the tradition of dilatory institutional support on this subject. One is also reminded of the federal requirement that institutions have in place drug abuse prevention programs—or plans for such programs—to qualify for federal funds for student aid (Education Act of 1965, Title IV). When compliance rests on an honor system, it is difficult to believe that programs are in every instance substantive.

A *meaningful* policy is notoriously difficult to contrive. A tenacious collegiate tradition of substantial alcohol use and misuse receives persistent support: consider the silver bullet shot by Coors, the ubiquitous Spuds MacKenzie, the paraphernalia spawned by other brewers. And the argument circulates that one cannot radically change a campus environment without threatening the applicant pool. When one adds—as one must in these times—the use of other drugs, the situation becomes even more difficult. The environment is still not eager for change.

A credible policy will articulate the main provisions of relevant state law and campus rules and detail enforceable sanctions that the institution indeed intends to enforce. Students and others are bright and quick to identify the irreducible core of regulation. They also know that the more stringent the regulation, the greater the need for their cooperation in its enforcement. Prohibition (though not my goal) in a campus of any size, for example, will very likely not be effective. (Curiously—and parenthetically—drug prohibition these days does not usually include reference to alcohol.) To promulgate such a rule in the face of all but inevitable violation may propose medicine as threatening as the disease.

A campus policy primarily targeted for students should also explicitly include provisions for troubled faculty and staff, an inclusion that reminds a community that alcohol and drugs do not pose problems for students alone.

A policy must be located within the context of the stated purposes of the institution. Brown no longer simply lists restrictive regulations; provisions are rooted in our *Tenets of Community Behavior*, designed to support an atmosphere conducive to learning and personal development. We speak of educational and counseling opportunities as much as strict regulation. In short, we have assumed the good will of the community, its essential health, and the aim of most to avoid confrontation with the law. Such an approach harmonizes with our approach to other matters. To maintain an arbitrary and ultimately unrealistic authority on drug matters alone seems out of proportion and inappropriate.

The creation of even the most rational policy is no panacea. Attitudes such as we have observed in top administrators undercut the most exquisite formulation. One dean congratulated his students on their altruism in purchasing liquor for the underaged when a raised drinking age left roughly three-fourths of the campus without legal access to alcohol. An administration must itself take its policies seriously and present them honestly and persuasively.

A drug policy that meets these conditions may generate support and cooperation more readily than if a consistent rationale and common interest are lacking. Further, when the issues are perceived broadly, and involve all members of the community, drug use and its implications are legitimized as a concern of more than a student life deanery.

In 1988–1989, for example, Brown asked faculty members and administrators, with upperclass partners, to serve as mentors to freshman residential units. These pairs oriented new students to liberal education and the specifics of our curriculum, and tolerance for genuine diversity and pluralism. In these orientations the corrosive impact on community norms was stressed for all drugs, e.g., in poor academic performance and diminished motivation, in the hurling of racial slurs or the expression of homophobic feelings, or in matters of vandalism or sexual assault. Individual responsibility was highlighted and techniques for intervention explained.

Undergraduate growth and development still include learning to cope with drugs, and especially alcohol. That development will almost surely not be in every instance untroubled. But perhaps in emphasizing the essential character of the institution and directly soliciting community support we can hope to change drinking norms more effectively than through a stern didacticism and angry prohibition.

A final word on enforcement. The college president whom we quoted at the outset remarks:

> The use of drugs in college is too deep a problem for colleges themselves to solve. . . . If colleges tried to expel all the students who use drugs, they would have to close their doors for lack of students. (Clark, p. 219)

Again, the tone is bleak and points to the broad social dimensions of the problem. I have heard one president lament that he is hostage to students who are abusive but without whom he would have no student body at all. These particular difficulties for some institutions are real.

"What happens when a law on the books is not enforced is that it gives students a tacit message that the world outside is not serious about the law, and that leads to a climate where underage drinking takes place" (*New York Times*, 1988). What has been said of the world beyond the ivory tower holds for the groves of academe as well. Perhaps more important, finally, is the general effect of unenforced prescriptions: when there is a lack of respect for one regulation, reduced credence in all the rest soon follows.

Academic Matters

In their review, "College Student Drinking Studies: 1976-1985," Saltz and Elandt (1986) note dryly: "Presumably, academic concerns are at the center of college students' lives. Despite this, our review of the literature failed to discover any article or report that seriously addressed the relationship between a student's drinking and his or her academic career. Instead, what knowledge we have is mostly limited to noting a relationship between drinking and grade-point average (GPA)" (p. 140).

One initiative at Brown focuses on students who have had significant difficulty with alcohol or another drug. Those students who are willing and able to acknowledge their problem as addiction, and to maintain abstinence, are on application granted adjustments in their academic progress such as reduced course load and more liberal arrangements for extensions.

This provision was first used with a student who, when contacted about his second—and usually final—academic dismissal, disclosed his residence in a drug treatment center. Following consultations with treatment staff, my colleagues and I determined that the student might return to school on strict probation.

The student, a junior, was expected to complete two courses from the prior semester, and attempt a reduced enrollment in the semester upcoming. He was also regularly to attend Anonymous meetings and a campus abstinence support group, and to meet with me to discuss his general adjustment and academic progress. The student met all required conditions, and went on, in fact, to be hired as a teaching assistant.

This success prompted standardization of the procedures under which he reentered the university. This policy has seemed beneficial. The guilt and shame of students who have manipulated faculty members and deans as well as the academic procedure, and otherwise violated the trust central to the academic enterprise, prevent them from seeking assistance with their academic progress, so undeserving and unworthy do they feel. The new policy, with its formal and impersonal stipulations, helps them to understand the institution's support of their changing lifestyle, and to avoid seeing its provisions as some sort of personal favor.

Since adoption of the policy, recovering students have been more candid about their chemical use, their academic self-esteem, and their responses to academic pressure. Conversations with such students have led to consideration of whether they are of a seriously academic nature; their reasons for attending college; the challenges of intellectual commitment; and the question of obligations to parents. These far ranging and introspective dialogues on academic matters are more significant questions, surely, than regularity of class attendance or GPA. And still other students have given abstinence a "trial run" on the basis of this policy.

It is hoped over the long term that this policy, together with a generally supportive atmosphere on campus and a burgeoning number of recovering individuals, will prompt those locked into drug use to reach out for help *before* they encounter serious academic difficulty. There is some indication that this is the case.

The policy has prompted other developments. Possible application of the policy retroactively has spurred questions on criteria. Whether abstinence should be the only response for a student covered by the policy also prompts new considerations. The seriousness of the policy in addressing substance abuse has led to more liberal application of medical leaves when students serially encounter drug-related difficulty. Finally, Brown has admitted several students because admission officers, and potential applicants, too, realize that the institution is supportive (*and* firm) with the addicted.

Debate on the policy was itself instructive, and provided new insights to those involved. The fact that the policy reveals a link between drug use and the academic side of college life has also prompted students to disclose their chagrin at faculty comments on "needing my fix at five" or laments that "too much acid as an undergraduate" accounts for classroom error. This seemingly innocuous banter, coupled with such things as an instructor's uncritical acceptance of the stereotype of the drunken artist, "inspired" by drink, suggest that consciousness raising among the faculty is in order. In short, just as an alternative beverage policy can have broad ripple effect in an institution, so the effects of this policy has led to the articulation of other concerns.

Faculty

Faculty members deserve attention because of their role in fostering campus tone, and because their familiarity with students may breed referrals. They can be encouraged to discuss alcohol-related phenomena in existing courses in their specialties, and institutional support might be found for this development. But faculty can also play a useful and important role in the rehabilitation of students even as they themselves make progress in recovery.

At Brown students, staff, and faculty regularly attend the same Anonymous meetings. They are included on the same referral list to answer confidential inquiries on drug use. Perhaps most interesting has been the bringing together of these same individuals in a luncheon group which allows everyone to feel appreciated, to practice social skills, to share cross-generational experiences, to see that addicts can lead full and useful lives, and to provide an informal support network across the campus (Donovan, 1989).

The Full Sweep: Sub-Freshmen to Alumni

I have discussed a broad policy designed to instill a "proper" sense of the role of alcohol and other drugs in a particular academic community, and described one initiative to increase intervention. I would like finally to provide some sense of the general character of the institution regarding alcohol and other drug programming.

Prior to matriculation students receive mailings on the drug policy, which is also discussed during Orientation. Parents, too, are reminded of institutional expectation, prevailing laws and social norms, as well as the significance of attitudes and behaviors that their sons and daughters will bring to campus with them. This message is reinforced at Orientation meetings and on Parents Weekend.

The campus, from faculty club to faculty home to fraternity to freshman dorm, is covered by a policy that requires the presence of non-alcoholic beverages wherever alcohol is served and which seems notably to have increased moderation. Drinking environments are closely monitored: entertainment of students by faculty, receptions for parents, the line of march at commencement, tailgating at the stadium.

Resident counselors to freshmen are trained in drug issues, as are a variety of other peer groups, including a corps of Drug and

Alcohol Resident Educators. A variety of one-shot "road show" presentations is offered by health educators. Social procedures for parties and for the service of food and drink are clearly articulated, and enforcement is frequently reviewed. Alternative drug-free entertainments have been encouraged, including an ambitious Weekend of Choice, wholly student sponsored, which focuses not so much on abstinence but self-conscious choice, and parties which feature elaborate video advertisements and a professional student disc jockey. A presence at the campus Health Fair and special events (e.g., the distribution of drug and sex information before spring vacation) also keep the issues alive. Outreach is attempted with minority students, women, and gays and lesbians. Special training events and guest speakers have been regularly arranged for athletes. Prominent notice is maintained of various drug-specific campus-based support groups. A group on stress and one on relationships are offered, as well as a group for family members of the addicted. Print material abounds. Press coverage is occasional but steady. Close liaison is maintained with Brown's Center for Alcohol and Addiction Studies, and with faculty members (e.g., in Anthropology and Psychology) whose interests are relevant. In short, whatever can be done is done to maintain full awareness of alcohol and other drug issues, including an ongoing discussion among colleagues on the various conceptions of alcohol problems and alcoholism.

A faculty and staff assistance program is watched closely. And alumni are kept abreast of developments in the alcohol and drug area through the alumni magazine. Efforts are made to foster a tone on alumni weekends which is consonant with the tone sought throughout the year. And when they are back for reunions, campus addicts and their significant others enjoy special meetings of the Anonymous groups which meet on campus through the year.

In sum, an effort is made to reach all populations through efforts at three levels of prevention. The task is big and must be renewed annually as community members come and go. Too, there is always need for new initiatives—more for graduate students, new thinking on treatment, more attention to faculty referrals. But as the years go by it is gratifying to see that progress can be made and that change is indeed possible (Block & Ungerleider, 1986).

References

Anderson, D. S., & Gadaleto, A. F. (1986). Continued progress: The 1979, 1982 and 1985 college alcohol surveys. *Journal of College Student Personnel 27*, 499-509.

Bloch, S. A., & Ungerleider, S. (1986). *The Brown University chemical dependency project: Final report—November 1, 1986.* Providence, R.I.: Brown University.

Boyer, E. L. (1987). *College: The undergraduate experience in America.* New York: Harper and Row.

Clark, A. Getting the most out of college. Unpublished manuscript.

Donovan, B. E. (1989). Campus-wide support for the chemically dependent: Common provision for faculty, staff and students. *Journal of Alcohol and Drug Education, 35.*

Donovan, B. E. (1981). Establishing a university alcohol program and some principles. *Journal of Alcohol and Drug Education, 27*, 62–77.

Gonzalez, G. M. (1980). The effect of a model education module on college students' attitudes, knowledge and behavior related to alcohol use. *Journal of Alcohol and Drug Eduction, 25*, 11.

Goodale, T. G. (1978). *A monograph on alcohol education and alcohol abuse prevention programs at selected American colleges*, coordinated by Office for Student Services, University of Florida, Gainesville, Florida, *32*, 611.

Journal of American College Health. (1987). Students, alcohol, and college health: A special issue, *36.*

Kinney, J., and Peltier, D. (1986). A model alcohol program for the college health service. *Journal of American College Health, 34*, 229–233.

Kraft, D. P. (1976). College students and alcohol. *Alcohol Health and Research World*, 10–14.

Kraft, D. P. (1984). A comprehensive prevention program for college students. In P. M. Miller and T. D. Nirenberg (eds), *Prevention of alcohol abuse.* New York: Plenum Press.

New York Times. (1988). Princeton eating club weighs alcohol policy. February 14.

Saltz, R., & Elandt, D. (1986). College student drinking studies: 1976–1985. *Contemporary Drug Problems, 13,* 117-159.

Straus, R., & Bacon, S. D. (1953). *Drinking in College.* New Haven, Conn.: Yale University Press.

FAMILY ISSUES
IN COLLEGIATE ALCOHOL USE,
MISUSE, AND TREATMENT

Barbara S. McCrady

Typically, we view the college student as away from his or her home and primarily influenced by peers rather than family. However, research data suggest that the family continues to have a direct impact on the behavior of college students, and that many college students have regular contact with their families. In this chapter, I will first consider the changing nature of the family in the late 1980s, and then discuss the impact of parents and peers on college student drinking. After considering these influences, I will discuss the general literature on marital and family therapy for substance abuse, and then consider the role of family therapy for treating college students with alcohol or drug problems. Finally, some alternative ways of treating collegiate substance abusers that involve other primary social networks will be addressed.

Changing Nature of the Family

In this last part of the twentieth century, the American family is in transition. No longer does the modal family have a working father that heads the household, a wife that tends to the home, and two children. Rising divorce rates, changing perspectives on marriage, economic pressures that require two incomes, and increased openness about homosexual relationships have radically changed the structure of the family. Therefore, when we discuss "the family," it is essential to specify what kind of family we are considering. There are a number of different and distinct family types in the United States: (1) married couples without children; (2) nuclear families consisting of two parents and children living in the same household; (3) remarried families, consisting of two married adults, with children from the current marriage and/or from the previous marriage of one or both partners, who may or may not be living in the same household; (4) multigenerational families living in the same household; (5) single parent families; (6) cohabitating heterosexual couples; (7) cohabitating same sex couples; (8) engaged or involved couples who do not live together; (9) long-term roommates without sexual involvement and, (10) adult offspring who have not yet married or formed a close bonded relationship and do not live in the parental household, but who still have living parents who are available or involved. Substance abuse problems may occur in an adult or child member of any of these family types.

College students have at least four different kinds of "families." They may have involvement with their family of origin, but also be heavily influenced by their friends and roommates on campus, and their boyfriend, girlfriend, or marital partner. Their drinking or drug use may also be markedly influenced by groups which they join, such as fraternities or sororities.

Impact of the Social Network on College Student Drinking

Parental and Family Influences

The family may influence collegiate drinking through several avenues: as a direct model of drinking behavior, as a means to transmit attitudes about alcohol, through expectations about drinking within the family context, and through the quality of the student's relationship to his or her family. Eight of ten studies (reviewed in Brennan, Walfish, & AuBuchon,

1986) which examined the relationships between parental and college student drinking behavior found a significant, positive relationship between students' reports of their parents' drinking and their own drinking. These relationships include: reported frequency of heavy drinking and intoxication (Fontane & Layne, 1979), beverage preference, at least among males (Fontane & Layne, 1979), and drinking frequency (Wiggins & Wiggins, 1987). Parental and student attitudes about alcohol have been found to be quite similar. Parents and sons or daughters report very similar reasons for drinking, including sociability, relaxation, fitting in with friends, and forgetting worries (Wilks & Callan, 1984). Student attitudes about alcohol also appear to be related to parental approval of the students' drinking (Brennan, Walfish, & AuBuchon, 1986).

Other aspects of students' relationships with their parents also appear to be related to drinking. Demographic characteristics of the parents, such as occupation or current marital status, appear unrelated to undergraduates' alcohol consumption (Friedman & Humphrey, 1985). However, contact with and closeness to family appear to be related to drinking. Students who count greater numbers of family members in their social support system tend to drink less (Fondacaro & Heller, 1983), and students who describe their families as highly cohesive are most similar to their parents in drinking practices (Wiggins & Wiggins, 1987). In general, perceived support from family is as predictive of drinking behavior as is perceived support from friends (Fondacaro & Heller, 1983). Surprisingly, many students perceive the family as a context in which they are expected to drink. About one-quarter of a group of students who felt that their drinking was affected by situational pressures reported that they felt that drinking alcohol was *expected* in their home (Fontane & Layne, 1979).

Peer Influences

While parental attitudes and behavior are correlated with college student drinking attitudes and behavior, stronger correlations are found between peer attitudes and behavior and student drinking. All reported studies which examined peer influence on drinking have reported a positive association between peer behavior and student drinking (Brennan, Walfish, & AuBuchon, 1986). Peer pressure to drink (Sherry & Stolberg, 1987), usual drinking of friends (quantity and frequency) (Wiggins & Wiggins, 1987), and friends' support for drinking (Liccione, 1980) are more strongly associated with collegiate drinking than are comparable measures of family behavior or attitudes. Other variables (summarized in Brennan, Walfish, & AuBuchon, 1986) positively associated with increased quantity or frequency of drinking include: involvement with a fraternity, involvement with a group of close friends who drink, and the presence of more friends in a drinking situation. The degree of social support that collegians receive from their friends does not appear to be related to student drinking, but is moderately associated with the experience of psychological symptoms (Fondacaro & Heller, 1983).

The above studies have relied on survey and self-report techniques to evaluate the influence of peers on drinking. Laboratory studies conducted with college students have examined the influence on student drinking of heavy or light drinking models. These studies suggest that men who are heavy drinkers tend to match their alcohol consumption to that of their drinking partner, whether the partner's consumption is heavy or light. The status of the model and interpersonal characteristics of the model also affect students' tendency to drink (Collins, Parks & Marlatt, 1985).

Overall, the literature is fairly clear in reporting a strong peer influence on collegiate drinking practices and an important, although somewhat less strong, family influence on student drinking and attitudes about alcohol. Given these two strong influences on student drinking, it would appear that treatment for college student substance abuse should consider family and relationship issues. In this next section, I will describe the traditional types of family-involved alcoholism treatments, and then will turn to a discussion of the application of these treatments to college students.

Marital and Family Approaches to Alcoholism Treatment

Marital and family approaches to alcoholism treatment have derived from three rather different perspectives: the disease model, behavioral models, and general systems theory. Each of these approaches, and treatment outcome studies derived from the approach will be discussed.

Disease Model Approaches

Contemporary disease model approaches describe alcoholism as a "family disease." This assumes that alcoholism is a physical, emotional/psychological, spiritual, and family disease (Cermak, 1986). Family members are seen as suffering from a disease, just as is the alcoholic. The disease of the family is labelled "co-dependence." Co-dependence is described as a "recognizable pattern of personality traits, predictably found within most members of chemically dependent families" (Cermak, 1986, p. 1). Most programs which provide family disease model treatment also draw from family systems models and stress that dysfunctional family roles, communication, and family homeostasis are important aspects of the family disease. Disease model based treatment programs usually include education about alcoholism as a disease, education about dysfunctional family behaviors which characterize the family disease, referrals to Al-Anon or Adult Children of Alcoholics groups, and individual or group therapy to focus on core personal and interpersonal issues. Many inpatient alcoholism treatment programs offer short-term residential treatment programs for family members.

Early studies of family disease model oriented treatment evaluated the effectiveness of separate group therapy for spouses of alcoholics. These studies generally reported better treatment outcomes for alcoholics whose spouses attended these groups than for those who did not (reviewed in Paolino & McCrady, 1977). There are few recent studies of this model. An evaluation of the family program at the Hazelden Foundation in Minnesota reported that participants showed positive attitudinal changes after the family treatment (Laundergan & Williams, 1979), and that 20 percent of the participants were more active in Al-Anon or Alateen than they had been prior to treatment (Laundergan, Shroeder & Barnett, 1980).

One recent study of Al-Anon reported that women with longer membership in Al-Anon used less negative coping, whether or not their husbands continued to drink (Gorman & Rooney, 1979).

Behavioral Perspectives

Behavioral perspectives assume an interdependence between drinking and family interactions. Interactions in alcoholic couples are viewed as reciprocal, with the behavior of each partner serving simultaneously as a cue to behavior of the other, and as a reinforcer of the partner's behavior. Research on alcoholic couples' interactions (McCrady & Hay, 1987) suggests that communication is characterized by negative and coercive interactions and a paucity of effective problem-solving skills. Couples' interactions appear to change when the alcoholic partner drinks, and some of the changes in interaction appear to be positive changes which may serve to reinforce the drinking behavior. Couples treatment based on behavioral models has focused on communication skills training, as well as interventions designed to increase the frequency of positive couple interactions.

Behavioral models have also viewed the partner as a potentially powerful source of reinforcement for the alcoholic. Behavioral models attend to the ineffective coping behavior of spouses of alcoholics, observing that many spouse behaviors actually may cue further drinking behavior, or inadvertently may reinforce the drinking (McCrady & Hay, 1987). Thus, a number of behavioral approaches focus on training spouses in new behaviors relevant to drinking. Some attention has been devoted to teaching spouses new behaviors for coping with the alcoholic's drinking, while other programs utilize the spouse as a source of reinforcement for therapy-relevant behaviors, such as taking disulfiram. Behavioral models have viewed alcoholism as maintained by multiple systems of reinforcement in addition to the family, and thus use individually oriented behavior change techniques for the alcoholic at the same time that marital therapy procedures are used.

Behavioral approaches have enjoyed less widespread popularity in the alcoholism treatment field, but behavioral clinicians have reported a number of well-controlled treatment outcome studies. Three major approaches to behavioral couples treatment have been taken: training for spouses to change behaviors related to drinking, use of spouses and others to reinforce treatment behaviors, and behavioral marital therapy techniques to change marital interactions.

Spouse Behavior Change Studies. No recent research studies have reported behavioral programs designed exclusively to change spouse behaviors, although some of the comprehensive behavioral marital therapy programs described below include spouse behavior change elements. An early study (Cheek et al., 1971) reported on a program to teach wives of alcoholics to modify the consequences of the alcoholic's drinking behavior and to become less distressed by situations with their partner that produced tension or anxiety. Only 17 of the 158 women offered the program agreed to participate, and only three attended more than five meetings. Post-tests revealed that the wives saw modest changes in their own and their spouse's behavior, especially in the area of communication. They reported no changes in drinking behavior.

A more recent approach to working with spouses (Thomas & Santa, 1982) describes a three component approach, focusing on (1) spouse coping with drinking and other life problems, (2) changing family functioning through therapy with the individual, and (3) using techniques to facilitate sobriety. Results suggest over the eighteen months after the initiation of treatment that 73 percent of the alcohol abusers decreased or stopped drinking and 57 percent entered treatment (Thomas, 1991; Thomas et al., 1987).

Use of Spouses as Reinforcers of Treatment. Two studies have reported on the effectiveness of spouse contracting in increasing compliance with taking disulfiram. The first of these studies (Azrin et al., 1982) reported on application of the community reinforcement approach to alcoholism in an outpatient setting. Subjects were randomly assigned to one of three experimental conditions: (1) *traditional treatment,* in which they were given a thirty-day prescription for disulfiram and an Antabuse booklet, and provided with five counseling sessions; (2) *disulfiram adherence,* in which clients brought their disulfiram to each session and took it in the presence of the counselor, were taught to take the medication at a set time and place, in the presence of a significant other, participation in role play in which the client might want to stop taking disulfiram or the partner might want to stop helping, and were instructed to call the counselor if noncompliant; (3) *behavior therapy plus disulfiram adherence,* which included the disulfiram adherence procedures, plus behavioral skills training in drink refusal, muscle relaxation, dealing with difficult social situations, identifying positive social and recreational activities, job-finding, and marital therapy.

Significant differences were found at the six-month followup. *Traditional* subjects reported an average of 16.4 drinking days in the previous month, compared to 7.9 for the *disulfiram adherence* group and 0.9 for the *behavior therapy plus disulfiram adherence* condition. Comparable results were reported for days of employment and days taking disulfiram in the previous month. Similar studies have also found support for the effectiveness of actively involving the spouse in disulfiram administration (Keane et al., 1984).

Behavioral Marital Therapy Studies. Two research groups have reported results of spouse-involved behavioral alcoholism treatment that addressed the marital functioning of alcoholic couples. Extensive clinical descriptions of these programs are available, and outcome data are beginning to be reported.

Project CALM (Classes on Alcoholic Marriages) (O'Farrell, Cutter, & Floyd, 1985), a couples aftercare program associated with an inpatient Veterans Administration alcoholism treatment program, was run as a controlled comparison of interactional and behavioral couples group therapy. Extensive data were collected to evaluate marital functioning, and drinking behavior. The only published empirical report of this project describes the outcomes immediately after treatment. Results suggested that couples in the behavioral condition showed significant improvements on marital satisfaction and marital communication, and that these improvements were significantly greater than the controls, and tended to be greater than the interactional group. Alcoholics in the behavioral marital group reported significantly less drinking days, when age and years of drinking problems were controlled across groups. No longer term follow-ups are yet available.

My own work has focused on identifying active components of spouse-involved outpatient alcoholism treatment (McCrady et al., 1986; McCrady et al., 1991). In the PACT (Project for Alcoholic Couples Treatment) study, male and female alcoholics were randomly assigned to one of three experimental groups: (1) a *minimal spouse involvement condition* (MSI), in which the spouse was present for all therapy sessions, but the focus of the sessions was on teaching the alcoholic behavioral skills to achieve and maintain abstinence; (2) an *alcohol-focused spouse involvement* (AFSI) condition, in which the alcoholic was taught skills for achieving and maintaining abstinence, and the spouse was taught skills to respond more effectively to drinking situations, and to abstinence, and (3) an *alcohol-focused spouse involvement plus behavioral marital therapy* (ABMT) condition, in which all the skills taught in the AFSI condition were included, as well as behavioral marital therapy techniques to enhance positive interaction and improve communication and problem-solving skills.

During treatment, there was a substantial dropout rate from the MSI condition, with less than 50 percent of subjects in that condition completing the treatment. The dropout rate from the other two conditions was less than 20 percent.

Over the eighteen months after treatment, an average follow-up of 93 percent was achieved. Data from the long-term follow-ups generally found that the ABMT couples had the most positive treatment outcomes. Marital satisfaction was higher in the ABMT group, there were substantially less marital separations, less negative and more positive affect was reported, and ABMT subjects showed a pattern of gradual improvement in the percent of abstinence days after treatment.

Overall, behavioral approaches have shown promise in alcoholism treatment. The three approaches described here, spouse treatment, using the spouse as an adjunct to treatment, and behavioral marital therapy, are quite different and may have different degrees of applicability to the college-age substance abuser.

Family Systems Perspectives

Family systems perspectives on alcoholism have incorporated many of the core concepts of family systems theory into models of the alcoholic family system. Steinglass's (1976) model posits that all families obey the general laws of all systems, including organization, homeostasis, circular causality of events, and feedback. Alcoholism is seen as an organizing principle in alcoholic families, and the presence or absence of alcohol is seen as the most important variable defining interactional behavior in the family. Research on the functioning of alcoholic families (Steinglass, 1979b; 1981) has found that these families have characteristically different patterns of interaction, depending on whether the alcoholic is abstinent, drinking, or in an unstable state of transition from drinking to abstinent or vice-versa. Drinking families and unstable, transitional families tend to have the most rigid patterns of behavior, while stable, abstinent families have the most flexible patterns of interaction.

Systems oriented treatment of alcoholic families utilizes a variety of techniques to affect interactions within the family. Therapy focuses on the interactional, rather than the individual level, and discussion of the presenting problem (drinking) is directed to a collaborative, interactional approach, rather than an individual approach. Attempts are made to redefine roles, realign alliances, and change patterns of communication within

the family. Understanding changes in family interactional behavior when the alcoholic is drinking is crucial to the therapy.

The only controlled study of family systems approaches to
alcoholism treatment compared individually oriented alcoholism treatment with couples treatment with and without a joint
hospitalization as part of the treatment (McCrady et al., 1979;
McCrady et al., 1982). Six-month results from the project
(McCrady et al., 1979) suggested that the two groups receiving
spouse-involved treatment had better outcomes in terms of
drinking than the individually oriented condition, but non-
parametric statistical analyses, required by the form of the distribution of the outcomes, did not allow direct comparison of
the experimental groups.

A four-year follow-up (McCrady et al., 1982) revealed no
statistically significant differences among the three groups.
However, trends suggested that the couples who participated in
the joint admission had somewhat fewer marital separations
or divorces, felt that their drinking status was better, had more
months of abstinence, and longer periods of continuous abstinence than couples in the other two conditions.

A second joint hospitalization study (Steinglass, 1979a),
more firmly grounded in family systems theory, provided a more
intense hospitalization experience. All couples first participated
in two weeks of thrice weekly multiple couples group therapy,
followed by a ten-day couples hospitalization where alcohol was
available, couples were closely observed and video-taped, and
daily couples groups were conducted. The hospitalization was
followed by three weeks of twice weekly outpatient couples
group, then six months of group meetings every six weeks.

No statistical analyses of the results were presented, but
descriptive data on the outcomes of eight of the ten couples
(nine alcoholics) were reported six months after treatment. One
subject was abstinent, four had decreased their drinking, and
three reported no change in amount consumed. However,
eight of the nine alcoholics had changed the pattern and context
of their drinking, and seven of the couples changed the pattern of
communication and resolution of marital conflicts.

The family systems area is one that has generated a great deal of enthusiasm in the alcoholism field, and family systems concepts have been incorporated into many programs. However, the empirical base for evaluating the effectiveness of this approach is lacking. The controlled studies to date have suggested little beyond demonstrating that intense couples-involved treatment is feasible, and may yield better outcomes than individually oriented treatment. Careful outcome studies that examine the process of family systems oriented treatment, and that compare the outcomes to appropriate control conditions, are simply lacking.

Family and Marital Approaches to Treating Collegiate Substance Abusers

This rather extensive review of marital/family approaches to alcoholism treatment leads to the question: "When are such approaches appropriate for the college student?" I think that family or couples therapy is strongly indicated in several situations. Clearly, the married student should be treated in a couples context whenever possible. Treatment probably should address issues for both partners related to coping with drinking, as well as concentrating on the couple's relationship. Since many college students who are married will have relatively new marriages, concentrating on communication and problem-solving skills is likely to improve the couple's chances of remaining together as well as dealing with the substance use.

Students who have regular contact with their families also are appropriate for family therapy, even if they do not live together. A number of studies (reviewed in Stanton & Todd, 1982) suggest that even young, hard-core drug addicts maintain regular family contact, and at least half continue to live with their parents, even as young adults. A variety of issues become the focus of family therapy with college substance abusers. Issues of autonomy and control, already important issues for young adults, become exaggerated by the substance abuse. Parents often attempt to regain control over their child's behavior, which creates conflict, and further distancing by the student. Parents may link their continued support to improvement in the substance abuse problem, or to improved academic achievement. They may insist that the student transfer to a college close to home, and require that he or she reside at home again. Resolving these kinds of family conflicts forms an important substrate for the substance abuse treatment.

A third situation which might indicate family therapy is that of the student who comes from a family where alcoholism is already present. At times, familial alcoholism only becomes apparent after family therapy has begun, while in other situations the student reports the family alcoholism at the beginning of treatment. The therapist must decide whether it is better to encourage the student's distancing from this family or to encourage a family focus to therapy.

For many collegiate substance abusers, family therapy is not possible due to distance from the family, or is undesirable. When this occurs, involvement of alternate types of social networks should be considered. As noted earlier in the chapter, friends' drinking behavior has a stronger impact on collegiate drinking than familial drinking and attitudes. The therapist could consider one of several types of treatments that involve the student's peer group on the campus. If the student is in a stable, long-term heterosexual or homosexual relationship, that partner could well be involved in the treatment. The partner's role could focus on support for changes in drinking behavior, contracting around the use of disulfiram, or improving the quality of the relationship itself.

Close friends might also be involved in the treatment. Friends would be able to provide better support to the substance abusing student if they were more knowledgeable about the kinds of changes the student was attempting to make. Contracts could be developed to facilitate support for change, and friends could learn to stop encouraging drinking or drug use.

Equally important for many students with severe alcohol or drug problems is developing an alternative social network that supports abstinence or moderated drinking. Some college alcohol assistance programs provide therapy groups for their clients, to facilitate accessing a different network. On some campuses, students have started Alcoholics Anonymous or Narcotics Anonymous groups, which become another source of support. In addition, students need to define activities that they find enjoyable, but that do not have a primary alcohol or drug focus.

Conclusions

Family and friends have a profound impact on the drinking and drug use of the college student. There are well-defined, family-involved treatments for substance abuse, which have some empirical support for their effectiveness. However, these models have not been systematically applied to the college substance abuser. The family treatments described in this chapter can readily be applied to many college students. For others, the clinician can think creatively in defining the student's current "family," and can modify and apply many of these approaches.

A Commentary on Conference Themes

The final section of this chapter will consider an important conference theme, "What are the reasonably noncontroversial, practical suggestions one can make to all university administrators regarding how model campus alcohol use programs might be conducted?" In partial answer to this question, the "Rutgers model" will be summarized.

Since 1980, Rutgers has been evolving a comprehensive approach to collegiate alcohol and drug use. This approach began well before I came to Rutgers in 1983, and much of the credit should be given to David Burns, who was the Assistant Vice-President for Student Life Policy and Services, as well as to two of my colleagues at the Center of Alcohol Studies, Drs. Gail Milgram and Rob Pandina. A number of other faculty and staff of the university are central to this model, including Dr. Robert Bierman, the medical director of Student Health Services, Dr. William Frankenstein, a former faculty member at the Center of Alcohol Studies who was very involved in the development of the partial residential concept which I will be describing, Lisa Laitman, who directs the Alcohol and Other Drug Assistance Program for Students, and Donna Spitzhof, who started the Alcohol and Other Drug Education and Training Program.

The Rutgers model included five major components: a comprehensive alcohol policy, an alcohol and drug education program, an alcohol assistance program for students, a partial residential facility for students with severe substance abuse problems, and a "recovering-housing" living option.

The alcohol policy was framed to develop a context for the responsible use of alcohol, in which use or nonuse would be equally accepted. The policy recognizes explicitly that students drink alcohol and takes no moral stand on this fact. The policy states that all parties must be registered with the university. Parties must be by invitation only, with a maximum of three guests per member of the group giving the party. One person must be designated as responsible for the party, and therefore would be liable if there were any untoward consequences. At any function where alcohol is served, no more that 50 percent of the budget can be spent on alcohol. Food and equally attractive, nonalcoholic beverages must be available. All beverages must be dispensed from the same location, so that students do not have to decide between the "alcohol line" and the "soft drinks line."

The committee that drafted the alcohol policy also recommended the development of alcohol education and alcohol assistance programs for the campus. The Alcohol Education and Training Program (AETP) was initiated in January 1983 and later became the Alcohol and Other Drug Education and Training program (ADETP). The goals of the program are (1) to encourage responsible decision-making about alcohol, (2) to promote responsible drinking behavior for those who choose to drink, and (3) to increase awareness of and respect for the choices and rights of non-drinkers. The ADETP provides workshops on several topics, including "Alcohol: Facts and Fiction," "Planning a Party? Things to Consider, " "Alcohol Advertising and You," "Is this 'Responsible drinking'?" "Drinking and Driving: What's your View?" and "Alcohol: Values and Responsibilities." These workshops are offered to residents of campus housing and to fraternities and sororities, but are not required. The ADETP has also provided a range of educational programs for residence life counselors, campus police, deans of students, members of the student counseling services, and academic advisors for the Economic Opportunity Fund programs.

A third component of the Rutgers model is the Alcohol and Other Drug Assistance Program for Students (ADAPS). ADAPS provides comprehensive outpatient services to students with alcohol or drug problems. Three types of referrals are accepted: self-referrals, voluntary referrals, and mandatory referrals. More than 80 percent of the students seen are either voluntary or self-referred.

As a direct outgrowth of the ADAPS, we opened a new, intensive treatment center in December 1988, the New Jersey Collegiate Substance Abuse Program (NJCSAP). A number of students seen through ADAPS had not been able to successfully change in an outpatient setting. Referrals to traditional inpatient settings were difficult, because most programs required a minimum twenty-eight–day length of stay, which almost guarantees that the student will lose a semester of college. To respond to this need, fifteen infirmary beds were reallocated to a small substance abuse treatment unit. Unfortunately, changes in insurance reimbursement and financial cutbacks in the university required us to close the unit in June 1993.

Students were referred to this program only if they had failed in outpatient treatment or had severe alcohol or drug problems. Lengths of stay and level of treatment intensity varied, depending on the needs of the student. Most importantly, the student remained on the campus, and was able to continue with course work. After an initial evaluation and orientation to the unit, the student was able to return to classes, while spending the remainder of his or her time on the unit. As the student progressed in treatment, he or she had planned time away from the unit. Much of this time allowed the student to test the skills taught during treatment, in environments that were high risk for drinking. Many students remained in residential treatment for a very brief stay and then entered recovery housing. They continued in intensive outpatient treatment at NJCSAP, coming in for several individual and group therapy sessions each week. When they completed treatment at NJCSAP, they were referred back to ADAPS. This was a unique model of treatment for college students. Because of the unusual nature of the program, a careful program evaluation was completed that examined traditional outcome measures, such as drinking and drug use, and nontraditional measures, such as retention in college, grade point average, and entry job after graduation. Results of the evaluation are currently being analyzed.

The final component of the Rutgers model is the recovery housing. Clearly, the university does not sanction alcohol and drug use in the dorms, but it occurs. In the fall of 1988, students became able to elect to live with other students in recovery from alcohol or drug problems. The dorm provides a social support network for abstinence. Students living in recovery housing receive continued support through NJCSAP or ADAPS, and must remain abstinent to retain this housing. This dorm arrangement is not designed for those students who drink in moderation, but it does address a need that abstinent students have voiced repeatedly.

In conclusion, one should not infer that the Rutgers model is ideal. Active, skills-oriented prevention programs are lacking, and the current policy is not uniformly enforced. However, the approach that Rutgers has taken to alcohol use is innovative and unique in its comprehensiveness.

References

Azrin, N. H., Sisson, R. W., Meyers, R., & Godley, M. (1982). Alcoholism treatment by disulfiram and community reinforcement therapy. *Journal of Behavior Therapy and Experimental Psychiatry, 13,* 105–112.

Brennan, A. F., Walfish, S., & AuBuchon, P. (1986). Alcohol use and abuse in college students. II. Social/environmental correlates, methodological issues, and implications for intervention. *International Journal of the Addictions, 21*, 475–493.

Cermak, T. (1986). *Diagnosing and treating co-dependence.* Minneapolis: Johnson Institute Books.

Cheek, R. E., Franks, C. M., Laucius, J., & Burtle, V. (1971). Behavior-modification training for wives of alcoholics. *Quarterly Journal of Studies on Alcohol, 32*, 456–461.

Collins, R. L., Parks, G. A., & Marlatt, G. A. (1985). Social determinants of alcohol consumption: The effects of social interaction and model status on the self-administration of alcohol. *Journal of Consulting and Clinical Psychology, 53*, 189–200.

Fondacaro, M. R., & Heller, K. (1983). Social support factors and drinking among college student males. *Journal of Youth and Adolescence, 12*, 285–299.

Fontane, P. E., & Layne, N. R. (1979). The family as a context for developing youthful drinking patterns. *Journal of Alcohol and Drug Education, 24*, 19–29.

Friedman, J., & Humphrey, J. A. (1985). Antecedents of collegiate drinking. *Journal of Youth and Adolescence, 14*, 11–21.

Gorman, J. M., & Rooney, J. F. (1979). The influence of Al-Anon on the coping behavior of wives of alcoholics. *Journal of Studies on Alcohol, 40*, 1030–1037.

Keane, T. M., Foy, D. W., Nunn, B., & Rychtarik, R. G. (1984). Spouse contracting to increase Antabuse compliance in alcoholic veterans. *Journal of Clinical Psychology, 40*, 340–344.

Laundergan, J. C., Shroeder, M. R., & Barnett, P. J. (1980). Family program client changes: A follow-up. *Alcoholism: Clinical and Experimental Research, 4*, 221.

Laundergan, J. C., & Williams, T. (1979). Hazelden: Evaluation of a residential family program. *Alcohol Health and Research World*, 1316.

Liccione, W. J. (1980). The relative influence of significant others on adolescent drinking: An exploratory study. *Journal of Alcohol and Drug Education, 26,* 55–62.

McCrady, B. S., & Hay, W. (1987). Coping with problem drinking in the family. In J. Orford (Ed.), *Coping with disorder in the family.* London: Croom Helm.

McCrady, B. S., Moreau, J., Paolino, T. J., Jr., & Longabaugh, R. L. (1982). Joint hospitalization and couples therapy for alcoholism: A four-year follow-up. *Journal of Studies on Alcohol, 43,* 1244–1250.

McCrady, B. S., Noel, N. E., Abrams, D. B., Stout, R. L., Nelson, H. F., & Hay, W. M. (1986). Comparative effectiveness of three types of spouse involvement in outpatient behavioral alcoholism treatment. *Journal of Studies on Alcohol, 47,* 459–467.

McCrady, B. S., Paolino, T. J., Jr., Longabaugh, R. L., & Rossi, J. (1979). Effects of joint hospital admission and couples treatment for hospitalized alcoholics: A pilot study. *Addictive Behaviors, 4,* 155–165.

McCrady, B. S., Stout, R. L., Noel, N. E., Abrams, D. B., & Nelson, H. F. (1991). Effectiveness of three types of spouse involved behavioral alcoholism treatment. *British Journal of Addiction, 86,* 1415–1424.

O'Farrell, T. J., Cutter, H. S. G., & Floyd, F. J. (1985). Evaluating behavioral marital therapy for male alcoholics: Effects on marital adjustment and communication from before to after treatment. *Behavior Therapy, 16,* 147–167.

Paolino, T. J., Jr., & McCrady, B. S. (1977). *The alcoholic marriage. Alternative perspectives.* New York: Grune & Stratton.

Sherry, P., & Stolberg, V. (1987). Factors affecting alcohol use by college students. *Journal of College Student Personnel,* July issue, 350–355.

Stanton, M. D., & Todd, T. C. (1982). *The family therapy of drug abuse and addiction.* New York: Guilford Press.

Steinglass, P. (1976). Experimenting with family treatment approaches to alcoholism, 1950-1975: A review. *Family Process, 15,* 97–123.

Steinglass, P. (1979a). An experimental treatment program for alcoholic couples. *Journal of Studies on Alcohol, 40,* 159–182.

Steinglass, P. (1979b). The alcoholic family in the interaction laboratory. *Journal of Nervous and Mental Diseases, 167,* 428–436.

Steinglass, P. (1981). The alcoholic family at home. Patterns of interaction in dry, wet, and transitional stages of alcoholism. *Archives of General Psychiatry, 38,* 578–584.

Thomas, E. J. (1991). Reaching the uncooperative alcohol abuser through a cooperative spouse: The unilateral approach. Presented at the NIDA National Conference on Drug Abuse Research and Practice, Washington, D.C., January.

Thomas, E. J., & Santa, C. A. (1982). Unilateral family therapy for alcohol abuse: A working conception. *American Journal of Family Therapy, 10,* 49–58.

Thomas, E. J., Santa, C., Bronson, D., & Oyserman, D. (1987). Unilateral family therapy with the spouses of alcoholics. *Journal of Social Service Research, 10,* 145–162.

Wiggins, J. A., & Wiggins, B. B. (1987). Drinking at a Southern university: Its description and correlates. *Journal of Studies on Alcohol, 48,* 319–324.

Wilks, J., & Callan, V. J. (1984). Similarity of university students' and their parents' attitudes toward alcohol. *Journal of Studies on Alcohol, 45,* 326–333.